DINOSAURS
OF THE ALBERTA
BADLANDS

DINOSAURS OF THE ALBERTA BADLANDS

Dr. W. Scott Persons IV
with illustrations by Dr. Julius T. Csotonyi

HARBOUR PUBLISHING

www.harbourpublishing.com

PAGE 1: What was that sound? As night falls, a *Pachycephalosaurus* stands alert and listening. But the noise it heard was only a little mammal scurrying about in the trees.

PAGES 2–3: See caption on pages 50–51.

FACING PAGE: Two crested hadrosaurs, *Saurolophus* and *Hypacrosaurus*, stroll out of a Cretaceous forest. A hungry raptor watches them pass. Each hadrosaur is over 9 metres long and 4 tons in weight. The raptor will have to wait for something smaller.

Harbour Publishing Co. Ltd.
P.O. Box 219, Madeira Park, BC, V0N 2H0
www.harbourpublishing.com

Photos by Amanda Kelley/Specimens at the University of Alberta except: page 36 photographer unknown; page 109 (all) courtesy Michael Burns; page 13 (top) reprinted from *An Encyclopedia of Canadian Biography*, Canadian Press Syndicate (Montreal, 1907); page 105 (top) courtesy Clive Coy; pages 6 (all), 7 (middle, middle circle inset, bottom), 24 (top), 27 (top right), 30, 31 (all), 32, 34 (inset, bottom), 35, 37 (all), 38 (all), 70 (top), 85 (top) courtesy Phil Currie; pages 128–29 (bottom) courtesy Greg Funston/Specimen in the Collections of the Royal Tyrrell Museum of Palaeontology; page 94 courtesy Mike Lieurance/UW-La Crosse; page 130 (middle, bottom) courtesy Ryan McKellar/Specimen in the Collections of the Royal Tyrrell Museum of Palaeontology; pages 7 (top, bottom circle inset), 12, 15, 20 (all), 21, 23 (left: Specimen in the Royal Ontario Museum; right: Specimen in the Houston Museum of Natural Science), 34 (top), 52, 66 (all; left: Specimen in the Carmen Funes Municipal Museum), 118, 119, 120, 135 courtesy Scott Persons/Specimens at the University of Alberta; page 110 (top) by Nick Stavrou/ Shutterstock.com; page 83 (top) courtesy Angelica Torices; page 128 (top) courtesy Aaron van der Reest; page 130 (top) by Lida Xing.

Models on page 119 courtesy Scott Persons; page 95 courtesy Eric Snively.

Illustrations on page 86 by Catmando/Shutterstock.com; page 69 by atsawin fugpan/Shutterstock.com; pages 66–67, 84, 92 by Herschel Hoffmeyer/Shutterstock.com; page 133 by JayPierstorff/Shutterstock.com; pages 11 (inset), 12, 41 (top), 42–43 (all), 44–45 (all), 57, 62, 76 (bottom), 78, 82, 91, 103 (top), 116, 121, 122 (all), 123 (all), 124 (all) by Nathan E. Rogers; pages 5, 9, 31, 52, 56, 108 (top) © Royal Tyrrell Museum of Palaeontology; pages 64–65 (bottom), 102–3 (bottom) by Stocktrek Images Inc./Alamy Stock Photo; pages 14, 26 by Warpaint/Shutterstock.com.

Edited and indexed by Brianna Cerkiewicz
Cover and text design by Diane Robertson
Cover images by Dr. Julius T. Csotonyi

Printed and bound in Canada

Canada Council   Conseil des Arts
for the Arts   du Canada

BRITISH COLUMBIA
ARTS COUNCIL
An agency of the Province of British Columbia

Harbour Publishing acknowledges the support of the Canada Council for the Arts, which last year invested $153 million to bring the arts to Canadians throughout the country. We also gratefully acknowledge financial support from the Government of Canada and from the Province of British Columbia through the BC Arts Council and the Book Publishing Tax Credit.

LIBRARY AND ARCHIVES CANADA CATALOGUING IN PUBLICATION

Persons, W. Scott, author

   Dinosaurs of the Alberta Badlands / Dr. W. Scott Persons IV with illustrations by Dr. Julius T. Csotonyi.

Includes index.

Issued in print and electronic formats.

ISBN 978-1-55017-821-0 (softcover).--ISBN 978-1-55017-822-7 (HTML)

   1. Dinosaurs--Alberta--Juvenile literature.
2. Badlands--Alberta--Juvenile literature. 3. Paleontology--Alberta--Juvenile literature.
I. Csotonyi, Julius, 1973-, illustrator II. Title.

QE861.9.C22A437 2018
j567.9097123   C2017-907497-0
                  C2017-907498-9

CONTENTS

DINO DIG SITES
ALBERTA

Philip J. Currie
Dinosaur Museum

★ 🏛

PIPESTONE CREEK BONEBED

LEGEND

★ Dinosaur Dig Sites

🏛 Museums

● Cities

ALBERTA

**DANEK
BONEBED**

EDMONTON

University
of Alberta
Paleontology
Museum

**DRY ISLAND
PROVINCIAL
PARK**

🏛
Royal Tyrrell Museum
of Palaeontology

CALGARY

 🏛
Dinosaur Provincial
Park Visitor Centre

Devil's Coulee
Dinosaur Heritage
🏛 Museum

**DINOSAUR
PROVINCIAL
PARK**

Introduction:

ALBERTA'S LOST WORLD

Alberta is the best place in the world to hunt for dinosaurs. More dinosaur species have been discovered in Alberta than anywhere else. Fossilized dinosaur skeletons from Alberta's **badlands** fill museums from New York to Los Angeles to Tokyo to London. I am one of many **paleontologists** who study the dinosaurs and other prehistoric animals that once roamed Alberta. Like all paleontologists, I want to be a time traveller.

The tyrannosaur *Gorgosaurus* lurks in the shadows around a Cretaceous watering hole. An armoured *Edmontonia* has come to drink, and so has a herd of duck-billed dinosaurs and kangaroo-sized pachycephalosaurs. The horned dinosaurs *Chasmosaurus* and *Styracosaurus* walk by. The *Styracosaurus* has spotted the predator.

A basking crocodile prepares to move out of the way. A large ceratopsian is coming through. But Alberta's prehistoric swamps were home to greater carnivores than crocs. In the background, an *Albertosaurus* eyes the horned dinosaur hungrily.

Imagine that, while standing in my research lab at the University of Alberta, we suddenly travel backwards 76 million years. We find ourselves in a very different place. The climate is warm and humid all year. All across the province, prairies and grasslands are replaced by forested swamps and flood plains. To the east, a shallow sea cuts North America in two. To the west, you might see the distant smoke of a volcano. Dragonflies, early birds and leather-winged reptiles called **pterosaurs** flit and swoop through the air. Turtles and crocodiles bask on sandy riverbanks and at the edges of swamps. Large herds of **herbivorous** dinosaurs graze on ferns and munch on tree leaves. In the shadows of the forests, there's a rustle. A pack of **carnivorous** dinosaurs is watching for a meal.

I wrote this book to help you understand and imagine what dinosaurs and their world were like. Alberta is so rich with **fossils** that it gives us the best glimpse into that world. We have learned a lot about the dinosaurs of Alberta, and new species are unearthed every year. Here, I have included the newest discoveries and the latest fascinating facts about the most amazing animals of all time.

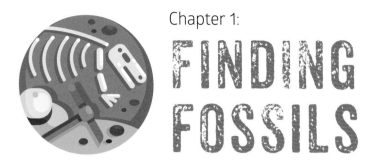

Chapter 1:

FINDING FOSSILS

Wetlands to Badlands
Alberta's Last 100 Million Years

Most of Alberta's dinosaur fossils come from 100 million to 66 million years ago, during a period of time called the **Late Cretaceous**. Late Cretaceous Alberta was a lush wetland where dinosaurs thrived. But there were

once lots of dinosaurs living in lots of habitats all over the world. Why are there so many dinosaur fossils in Alberta? The secret to Alberta's dinosaur treasure trove lies in a series of lucky events. It began with the rise of mountains in the west.

The Rocky Mountains started to form around 80 million years ago. Rivers flowing down the young mountains picked up **sediments** (dirt, sand and ground-up rock) and carried them to the eastern lowlands. Some of these sediments buried fallen logs, footprints in mud and the skeletons of

The duck-billed dinosaur *Parasaurolophus* stands on the shore of North America's inland sea. In the distance, the dead body of another duckbill rots in the hot salty air. The dead duckbill's bones will sink into the sand and be buried. Eventually, these bones will fossilize.

It was a wetter world 80 million years ago. Sea levels were high and a waterway cut North America in two.

CRETACEOUS

The articulated tail of a duck-billed dinosaur awaits excavation on a hilltop in the Alberta badlands.

Fifteen thousand years ago, it was really cold! Ice age glaciers covered much of the land.

QUATERNARY

dead animals. Once protected underground, these logs, footprints and bones eventually became fossils. Over millions of years, many dinosaur skeletons and other fossils built up layer by layer in the ancient ground of Alberta. As time rolled on, the dinosaurs went extinct and more sediments piled up. The mountains kept rising, the climate cooled and the inland sea shrank to today's Gulf of Mexico. Alberta's dinosaur fossils were buried deep in the earth, where they were protected for tens of millions of years.

Roughly 15,000 years ago, the ice came. During the great ice ages, massive glaciers covered much of Alberta. These glaciers slowly scraped across the land like giant bulldozers. They removed much of the sediments that covered the fossil layers. Then the ice melted. The glacial meltwater and a few more thousand years of **erosion** by wind and rain finished the work. Dinosaur-age layers were then revealed across Alberta—just in time for paleontologists to find them.

#1 Namesake
Tyrrell's Tyrannosaur

Joseph Tyrrell (TEER-uhl) was a **geologist**—a scientist who studies rocks and the natural forces that shape our planet. He was also an adventurer who explored much of Alberta's unmapped badlands. One day in 1884, he was studying the badlands and found a huge skull. Tyrrell recognized the skull as a dinosaur fossil. This was important! No dinosaur had ever been found in Alberta before. Carefully, he dug up the skull and wrapped it in cloth. But he had a problem. There was no dinosaur museum in Alberta and no paleontologist to study the skull. So Tyrrell took his find

Joseph Tyrrell was one of Alberta's first dinosaur hunters. He discovered an *Albertosaurus* skull in 1884.

The skeleton of *Tyrannosaurus* looms over visitors at the Royal Tyrrell Museum of Palaeontology.

on a week-long journey to Calgary. Then it was shipped by train to Ottawa. Eventually, it travelled all the way to New York City and the American Museum of Natural History. Scientists discovered that Tyrrell's skull belonged to a new species of dinosaur. It was a relative of *Tyrannosaurus* and was named *Albertosaurus*.

Today, fossils discovered in Alberta do not have to travel nearly as far. There are museums and research stations across the province. One of these museums is called the Royal Tyrrell Museum of Palaeontology. It's located smack-dab in the middle of the badlands. It sits only a few kilometres from where Tyrrell found his skull.

ALBERTOSAURUS

PRONUNCIATION:
AL-ber-toh-SAWR-us

MEANING: Alberta lizard
AGE: Late Cretaceous,
71–68 million years ago
HABITAT: Flood plains and wetlands
DIET: Other dinosaurs

11
metres
long

├──── 14m ────┤

In the badlands of Alberta, you can see rock layers stacked one on top of another.

Telling Time
How Scientists Age the Earth

Rock layers tell the story of a planet's past. New rock layers slowly form on top of old ones. As they do, fossils may be preserved inside them. How do scientists know how old a fossil is? They check what rock layer it came from. Old rock layers are buried underneath younger rock layers. If you find fossils in two different layers, the fossils from the higher layer are younger. But how do you know the actual age of any one layer? Scientists use a method called **radiometric dating**. Some rocks are radioactive. This means some of the super tiny atoms that make them up are unstable. These atoms break apart over time. The more time that has passed since the rock layer formed, the more of its atoms will have broken apart. So scientists can figure out a layer's age by looking at how many of these atoms are broken.

Bones of Stone
How Fossils Form

A fossil is an object from the past that tells us about pre-historic life. A fossil doesn't have to be an actual piece of an animal or plant. It just needs to show some proof that prehistoric life was around. There are many different kinds of fossils. They can form in many different ways. Fossils can be footprints or burrows left in hardened mud. They can be ancient plants buried and squeezed into lumps of coal by the weight of the ground above. They can even be entire bodies frozen in ice or trapped in **amber**. But by far the most common kind of dinosaur fossils are **mineralized** bones.

Your bones are alive. They are filled with growing flesh, squishy fat and flowing blood. They are also made of hard minerals. These minerals make your bones strong enough to support your body and protect your internal organs. When an animal dies, most of its soft body rots. Even the living parts of its bones. But the hard minerals in the bones can last. If a skeleton is buried and remains safe underground, the minerals in the bones can stay just as they are for millions of years.

A buried bone is filled with holes where the flesh, fat and blood used to be. Water in the ground can seep into those holes. This water sometimes carries small amounts of other minerals from the ground. Slowly, these ground minerals can fill the empty spaces in the bones. Eventually, the water dries. The ground minerals inside the bone harden together into rock. This process is called **mineralization**. When this happens, the buried bones become much heavier and often change colours. But the original bone minerals are still there. This is why it's true to say that the fossil skeleton of a dinosaur is both bone and rock. It's made of both.

Preservation Potential
Why Some Things Fossilize Better Than Others

Lots of animals don't have much chance of being preserved as fossils. Bones and shells are common fossils because they're made of hard minerals. Animals with no hard parts—like jellyfish or slugs—usually just rot. Clams and mussels have a very high chance of becoming fossils. They have hard shells and usually live in small sandy burrows. Often they die inside their burrows, so they are already buried.

In rock layers of ancient river bottoms, clam and mussel shells are common fossils.

Actual Size

PREHISTORIC POOP

Rarely, soft things can be fossilized...even poop. A chunk of fossilized poop is called a **coprolite**. Don't worry, after millions of years and complete mineralization, coprolites don't smell. But they can show what prehistoric animals ate. Coprolites from herbivores may be filled with fossilized seeds or small pieces of wood. Coprolites from carnivores may contain bone fragments.

Actual Size

BROKEN EGG

These pieces belong to a dinosaur egg discovered in Alberta's Dinosaur Provincial Park. The dinosaur that laid the egg probably weighed several tons. But if the egg were put back together, it would be smaller than a cantaloupe. Dinosaur eggs are often gigantic in cartoons and movies, but that's wrong. No dinosaur egg was much larger than a basketball. The baby dinosaurs that hatched from them were about the size of house cats.

Actual Size

Big and Scaly

Many dinosaurs had skin covered with hair-like feathers. The hairy coats of mammals and the feathery coats of dinosaurs trap and hold in body heat. But other dinosaurs had scaly hides. This dinosaur skin fossil is from a **hadrosaur** (a duck-billed dinosaur). You can easily see the skin's scales. Many very large dinosaurs had featherless skin like this.

Poop!

Large animals that live in warm climates don't need heavy coats. They stay warm thanks to their large bodies. Today's largest mammals (such as elephants, rhinos, hippos and water buffalo) also don't have very much hair. Large scaly dinosaurs may have had a few feathers for decoration. They may have also had eyelash-like feathers on their faces.

What would it be like to pet a dinosaur? This skin fossil shows that duck-billed dinosaurs were covered in lumpy scales.

Actual Size

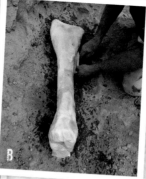

First, paleontologists uncover the leg bone of a duck-billed dinosaur (A). Then they wrap it in wet paper towels (B). Then cloth soaked in plaster (C). In the hot summer sun, the plaster will dry quickly. The bone can then be safely carried away.

Safe Travels
Digging Up and Transporting Dinosaur Bones

Although large fossil bones are mineralized and hard, they are also often fragile. If you don't handle them carefully, they may break. This makes digging up (**excavating**) and moving big fossils tricky. To keep fossils safe, paleontologists use a method called jacketing:

1. Paleontologists uncover the top and dig around the sides of the fossil. They don't move the fossil but leave it sitting in the ground instead.

2. They add a layer of soft material that sticks closely to the fossil. This material can be anything from wet paper towels to aluminum foil to old newspaper.

3. They cover the fossil with strips of burlap soaked with plaster. Once the plaster has dried, it forms a protective jacket. The jacket covers the fossil like a cast over a broken bone.

4. They dig out the bottom of the fossil and flip the fossil over. The bottom gets covered in a jacket too.

5. The fossil is ready to be safely lifted and carried away.

Sometimes, lifting and carrying a dinosaur fossil and its plaster jacket is easier said than done. Parts of a dinosaur's skeleton (often the skull and hips) can be so big that even 10 or more paleontologists cannot pick them up. When our team at the University of Alberta is faced with such heavy fossils, we call in a dinosaur airlift. We wrap the fossil in a net and tie the net to the rescue cable of a powerful helicopter. It then flies the fossil up and away.

A helicopter uses a net and rescue cable to lift the jacketed skull of a *Styracosaurus.*

Fossil preparator Howard Gibbins carefully picks away at a dinosaur bone in the University of Alberta fossil laboratory.

A Bone to Pick
Cleaning Dinosaur Bones

After a dinosaur bone is dug up in the badlands, there is still a lot of work to do. Inside the jacket, hard rock still clings to the bone. Before paleontologists can study the new find, this rock must be removed. The fossil may also be very crumbly. Crumbly bone must be hardened using special glue. Often, a dinosaur bone is found broken into many small pieces. These pieces need to be put back together. All these jobs are too delicate to do in the field. They are done in a laboratory by trained people called fossil **preparators**. Preparators must work very carefully, so they don't use big tools, like shovels or pickaxes. Instead, they use paintbrushes, small chisels and dental picks (the same thin metal tools a dentist uses to clean your teeth). How long does all this take? Usually, preparators will work for triple the time that it took to excavate the fossil in the field.

Fossil preparators use paintbrushes and dental picks to clean fossils.

This is the tail of a duck-billed dinosaur on display at the Royal Ontario Museum. Notice how every bone is held in place by a metal support.

The skeleton of *Tyrannosaurus* posed attacking an armoured nodosaurid.

Star Attractions
Dinosaur Bones in Museums

Most dinosaur bones in a museum are not on display. Instead, they are stored in a large vault. There, paleontologists can study them easily. However, when a museum does decide to put a dinosaur skeleton on display, it's a lot of work. Fossilized bones are heavy and fragile. The museum must build special metal braces to hold each bone in place.

It's very rare to find a whole dinosaur skeleton. Usually, at least a few bones are missing. Most museum skeletons are actually incomplete. But museums often want to fill in these missing pieces. That way, their visitors can see and understand the dinosaur's full shape. Paleontologists can create models of missing bones by looking at the bones of closely related dinosaurs. These model bones complete the skeleton. But it is important to remember that the replicas are only a best guess at what the bones actually looked like.

Museums also have to decide how to pose the skeleton. Paleontologists must think hard about how the dinosaur could move. They must decide on a body position that's both realistic and exciting to look at.

DINO DIG SITE:
DANEK BONEBED

A BED THAT'S JUST RIGHT

Sometimes, a lot of fossils are discovered all at once. An area filled with lots of fossil bones is called a **bonebed**. Small bonebeds can be only half a metre across. They may contain the bones of only a few animals. Other bonebeds can extend for tens or even hundreds of metres. They can contain the skeletons of many different prehistoric animals. It takes a long time to excavate big bonebeds. Paleontologists return to dig at these sites year after year.

Excavations at the Danek Bonebed reveal the bones of both large adult and small young *Edmontosaurus*.

DINO CSI

Every summer for the past nine years, a research team from the University of Alberta has excavated fossils from the Danek Bonebed. We have found more than 600 bones at the site! Each bone is a new clue to figuring out what created this extraordinary mass dinosaur grave. We can now piece the mystery together.

FLOCKING TOGETHER

The Danek Bonebed is strange. Nearly all its bones belong to one kind of dinosaur, the duck-billed *Edmontosaurus*. *Edmontosaurus* was a common Albertan dinosaur, but many other species lived alongside it. A good dinosaur detective can reach only one conclusion. The Danek Bonebed is not random.

Sometimes, flowing water can sort dead animals by size. A fast-flowing river can sweep away the floating dead bodies of even large animals. But as a river slows, it loses energy and its flow weakens. It may still be strong enough to carry the bodies of small animals but will stop carrying larger bodies. This can lead to animals of one size getting dropped off all together in one place. Is that what happened at the Danek Bonebed? No. Although the Danek Bonebed is almost completely made up of *Edmontosaurus* bones, these bones come from both huge adults and much smaller pony-sized juveniles (not fully grown animals). Juvenile and adult *Edmontosaurus* probably lived together in herds. The Danek Bonebed likely formed when one of these herds met with a sudden disaster. Perhaps the *Edmontosaurus* herd was wiped out by a hurricane.

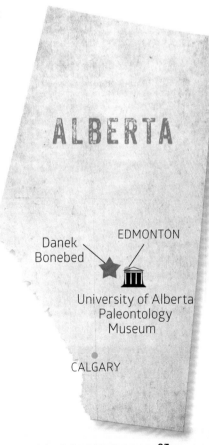

ALBERTA

Danek Bonebed

EDMONTON

University of Alberta Paleontology Museum

CALGARY

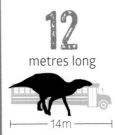

12
metres long

—— 14m ——

EDMONTOSAURUS

PRONUNCIATION: ed-MON-toh-SAWR-us

MEANING: Lizard of the Edmonton Formation
AGE: Late Cretaceous, 73–66 million years ago
HABITAT: Coastal marshes and flood plains
DIET: Plants

A CARNIVORE'S CALLING CARD

A mass of dead duckbills was bound to attract **scavengers**. Many bones from the Danek Bonebed have been munched on. Marks on the surfaces of the bones record where sharp teeth cut across them. Who was scavenging the carcasses? Paleontologists have found crocodile teeth next to the *Edmontosaurus* bones, so crocodiles were among the feasters. However, most of the tooth marks show scratch patterns

Crunch! These deep cuts are the bite marks of a tyrannosaur.

A large tyrannosaur tooth was discovered among the duckbill bones. The tyrannosaur must have been feeding.

Paleontologists found this crocodile tooth mixed in with the *Edmontosaurus* bones in the Danek Bonebed.

that could be left only by large teeth with **serrated edges.** The teeth of **tyrannosaurs** fit this pattern. Teeth from the tyrannosaur *Albertosaurus* have also been found at the site. Still, most of the bones don't have tooth marks and weren't scavenged. The sudden death of so many *Edmontosaurus* seems to have created more meat than even hungry crocodiles and tyrannosaurs could eat.

SHED VS. DEAD TEETH

Look carefully at these two tyrannosaur teeth. The tooth on the right was found in the jaws of a nearly complete tyrannosaur skeleton. It was still sitting in its socket. It's what we call a "dead tooth," because it comes directly from a dead body. The tooth on the left was found mixed in among the hadrosaur bones of the Danek Bonebed, with no other tyrannosaur fossils nearby. It's a **shed tooth.** Like modern sharks and crocodiles, dinosaurs replaced their teeth often. New teeth grew up from below old ones. When old teeth became worn out, new teeth were ready to replace them. Compare the tips of the two teeth, and you will see that the shed tooth on the left has a worn tip.

The part of a tooth that sticks out of the gums is called the crown. The part of a tooth below the gums that holds it in the jaw is called the root. When it was time for a worn-out tooth to be shed, the old tooth's root would be absorbed by the gums. The same thing happens when we humans lose the roots of our baby teeth as our adult teeth grow in from below. You can see that the dead tooth on the right looks larger than the shed tooth on the left. The dead tooth still has a long

In this *Daspletosaurus* jaw you can see a new tooth growing in underneath an old one.

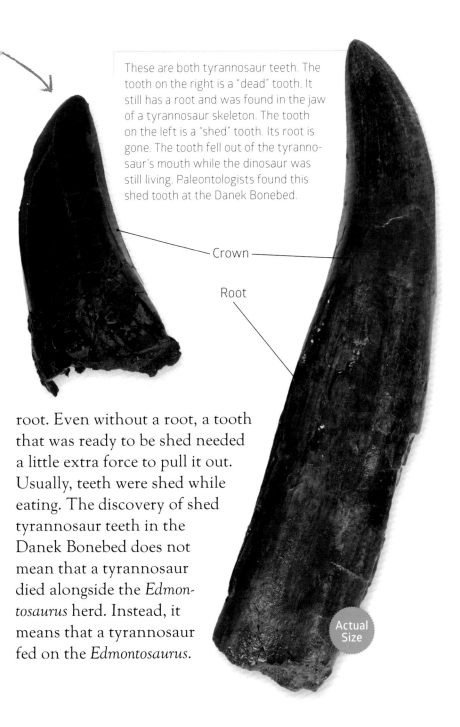

These are both tyrannosaur teeth. The tooth on the right is a "dead" tooth. It still has a root and was found in the jaw of a tyrannosaur skeleton. The tooth on the left is a "shed" tooth. Its root is gone. The tooth fell out of the tyrannosaur's mouth while the dinosaur was still living. Paleontologists found this shed tooth at the Danek Bonebed.

Crown

Root

Actual Size

root. Even without a root, a tooth that was ready to be shed needed a little extra force to pull it out. Usually, teeth were shed while eating. The discovery of shed tyrannosaur teeth in the Danek Bonebed does not mean that a tyrannosaur died alongside the *Edmontosaurus* herd. Instead, it means that a tyrannosaur fed on the *Edmontosaurus*.

ALL AJUMBLE

The Danek Bonebed contains no articulated skeletons. An articulated skeleton is a skeleton with all its bones still arranged next to each other the way they were in life. In the Danek Bonebed, all the bones are disconnected. They're mixed together like a well-shaken jigsaw puzzle. This makes it difficult to figure out which bones belonged to which skeletons. But it tells us something important about the history of the site. To stay articulated, a skeleton must be buried quickly, before the flesh that holds it together has rotted. The Danek jumble paints a gruesome picture: a mass of dead *Edmontosaurus* rotting away until their skeletons fell apart. The bones were then probably washed a short distance away by a surging river. This mixed all the bones up but did not sort them by size. Instead, the bones sank in the swampy water, where they were buried and fossilized.

Scattered ribs (A), leg bones (B) and vertebrae (C) cover the Danek Bonebed.

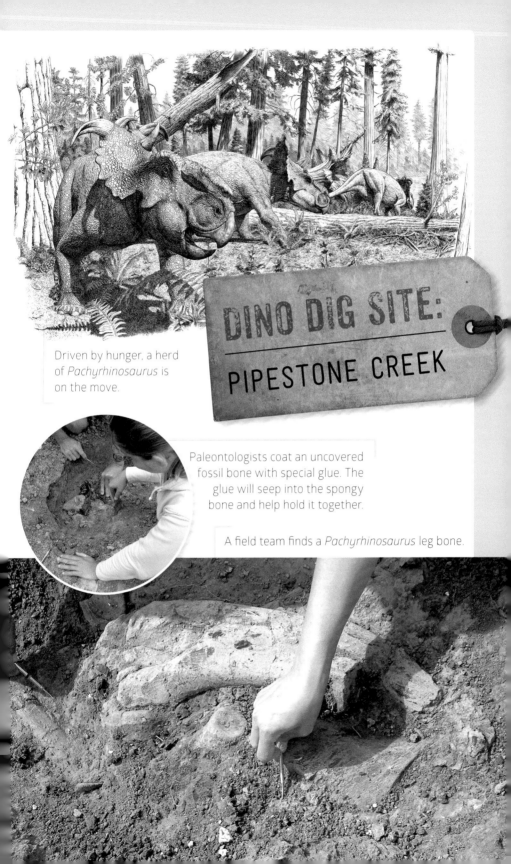

Driven by hunger, a herd of *Pachyrhinosaurus* is on the move.

DINO DIG SITE:
PIPESTONE CREEK

Paleontologists coat an uncovered fossil bone with special glue. The glue will seep into the spongy bone and help hold it together.

A field team finds a *Pachyrhinosaurus* leg bone.

A dig team works away at the Pipestone Creek Bonebed. Buried in the hillside are the skeletons of a *Pachyrhinosaurus* herd.

ALBERTA

Pipestone Creek Bonebed

Philip J. Currie Dinosaur Museum

EDMONTON

CALGARY

MASS MOVEMENT

The Pipestone Creek Bonebed contains the jumbled fossils of more than 25 *Pachyrhinosaurus* skeletons. *Pachyrhinosaurus* was a kind of **ceratopsian** (horned dinosaur). It was about the size of a modern white rhinoceros. Great herds of such large herbivores must have eaten a tremendous amount. They would have left trails of destroyed plant life wherever they went. *Pachyrhinosaurus* herds probably couldn't stay in one place for very long, or they'd run out of food. Paleontologists think these dinosaurs migrated over long distances, grazing as they went. Modern large herding herbivores, such as bison, caribou and wildebeest, also migrate to find food. During **migrations**, these modern animals often have to cross dangerous rivers to reach good feeding grounds. This can be a disaster. Thousands of animals may drown. Others may be trampled by panicking members of their own herd! Many paleontologists think this is what happened to the Pipestone Creek *Pachyrhinosaurus* herd.

8
metres long

14m

PACHYRHINOSAURUS

PRONUNCIATION: PACK-ee-RYE-no-SORE-us

MEANING: Thick-nosed lizard
AGE: Late Cretaceous, 73–69 million years ago
HABITAT: Flood plains and coastal marshes
DIET: Plants

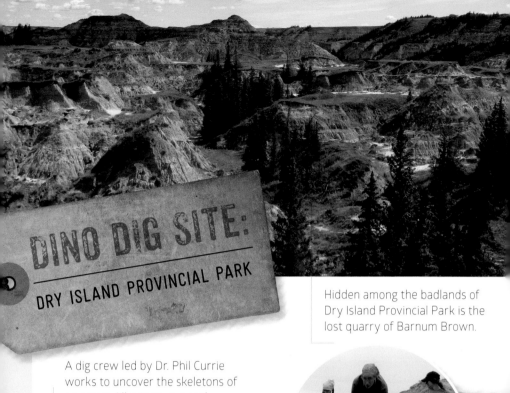

DINO DIG SITE:
DRY ISLAND PROVINCIAL PARK

Hidden among the badlands of Dry Island Provincial Park is the lost quarry of Barnum Brown.

A dig crew led by Dr. Phil Currie works to uncover the skeletons of an entire *Albertosaurus* pack.

The bones of an *Albertosaurus* stick out of the rocks at the Dry Island Bonebed. More than 20 *Albertosaurus* died together at this spot, 70 million years ago.

ALBERTA

EDMONTON

Dry Island Provincial Park

CALGARY

Royal Tyrrell Museum of Palaeontology

Dr. Philip Currie
Rediscovering a Tyrannosaur Graveyard

Monospecific bonebeds are fossil sites filled with many bones of only a single species of dinosaur. Monospecific bonebeds, like Danek and Pipestone Creek, tell us that many species of herbivorous dinosaurs often died together in big groups. This means they probably also lived in groups. What about the predatory dinosaurs? A monospecific bonebed in Alberta's Dry Island Provincial Park has shown that tyrannosaurs were some of the most social carnivorous dinosaurs.

The famous paleontologist Barnum Brown found the Dry Island Bonebed in 1910. At the site, Brown excavated fossils from several skeletons of the tyrannosaur *Albertosaurus*. He shipped these fossils to the American Museum of Natural History in New York City. Unfortunately, although Barnum Brown was an excellent fossil hunter, he took lousy notes. With no maps, it was impossible for later paleontologists to find the Dry Island Bonebed and continue Brown's work. But the American Museum of Natural History had asked Brown to take photos of his excavations to use in their exhibits. Nearly 100 years after Brown discovered the site,

CONTINUED ON NEXT PAGE

Paleontologist Barnum Brown hunted for fossils across Canada and the US. He is most famous for discovering the first skeleton of *Tyrannosaurus rex*.

Dr. Phil Currie tried to find the bonebed again. He inspected the photos and noticed a ridge with a line of tall spruce trees growing on it. Dr. Currie hiked through Dry Island Provincial Park with the photo in hand. After several days of searching, he found that ridge with the trees. The bonebed was rediscovered!

It turned out that Barnum Brown had only scratched the surface. New excavations at the Dry Island Bonebed uncovered a trove of tyrannosaur bones. Just how big was a tyrannosaur pack? Dr. Currie and his team found bones from at least 23 *Albertosaurus*. Some were young juveniles, and some were mature adults. Why did tyranno-saurs form such large groups? Big packs may have been needed to attack large herds of herbivorous dinosaurs. The packs may also have been close family groups. By banding together, these families could defend the best hunting territory from rival groups.

The badlands of Dinosaur Provincial Park are beautiful. They also hold a treasure trove of fossils.

DINO DIG SITE:
DINOSAUR PROVINCIAL PARK

In Dinosaur Provincial Park, you can find very small fossils just sitting on the ground. To collect these tiny treasures, paleontologists have to get low and crawl across the badlands. (I'm the one on the left in the green hat.)

It takes a lot of plaster to cover big bones.

The skeleton of a raptor is exciting find. But to get it c you have to break through rock and shovel a lot of dir

WORLD CLASS

In 1979, Alberta's Dinosaur Provincial Park became a UNESCO World Heritage Site. It earned this honour thanks to the importance of its fossils and the beauty of its badlands. Dinosaur Provincial Park spans more than 73 square kilometres (larger than 45,000 pro hockey rinks). In much of the park it's impossible to take a step in any direction without stepping on a fossil. The park is filled with fossil wood, dinosaur footprints and lots of fossil bones. These bones are preserved in many different ways. There are **microsites**, monospecific bonebeds, single bones and fully articulated skeletons.

ALBERTA

EDMONTON

Dinosaur Provincial Park Visito Centre

Dinosaur Provincial Park

CALGARY

SMALL WONDERS

Take a look at this pile of little fossils. There are crocodile teeth, fish scales, **vertebrae** from **champosaurs**, turtle shell fragments and dinosaur teeth. All these fossils were found fewer than four metres away from one another. Collecting them all took less than an hour. Such rich spots loaded with small fossils are called microsites. Paleontologists think microsites formed after ancient riverbanks collapsed. A steep riverbank can be made of sediments that have piled up over many years, along with many years' worth of buried bones. When the bank collapses, all that sediment and bone drops into the flowing water. The water may then carry away the small bones and dump them all together on a downstream sandbar. Microsites usually contain the skeletal remains of many small animals and a few small fossils (like teeth or finger bones) of large animals. These rich and diverse fossil sites are extremely useful to paleontologists. They help us understand what ancient **ecosystems** were like.

These little fossils were all dug up in the same spot—a place called a microsite. These bones and teeth come from more than 10 different species, including turtles, fish, champsosaurs, crocodiles, tyrannosaurs, raptors and many different herbivorous dinosaurs.

NEW SPECIES!

Fossil collectors have been combing the badlands of Dinosaur Provincial Park since 1898. But there are always more spectacular specimens and new discoveries. In the spring of 2014, paleontologists discovered a brand-new species of horned dinosaur. They named it *Mercuriceratops*. In many ways, *Mercuriceratops* looks like other species of horned dinosaurs that have also been discovered in the park. But its neck shield is shaped differently. This shield proves that it's a new species.

Sometimes, new dinosaur species are discovered not in the field but in museums. In 1982, a set of small hip bones was dug up in Dinosaur Provincial Park. At the time, paleontologists didn't know what kind of animal the hip bones belonged to. So they put the bones into storage. Many years later, new paleontologists took a look at the bones. They realized that they belonged to a new type of small meat-eating dinosaur. They named it *Hesperonychus*. It was a relative of *Velociraptor*. *Hesperonychus* was a good climber and lived in the park's now-fossilized forests.

This is the hip bone of a new dinosaur species, *Hesperonychus*. Most of the rest of the skeleton is missing.

Actual Size

MERCURICERATOPS

PRONUNCIATION:
mer-kur-i-SEH-rah-tops

MEANING: Mercury-horned face
AGE: Late Cretaceous,
77 million years ago
HABITAT: Wetlands
DIET: Plants

6
metres
long

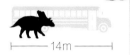

├─────── 14m ───────┤

HESPERONYCHUS

PRONUNCIATION:
HESS-peh-RO-NIH-cuss

MEANING: Western claw
AGE: Late Cretaceous,
76.5 million years ago
HABITAT: Swamps
DIET: Small reptiles, birds, fish
and mammals

1
metre
long

├───── 6m ─────┤

Chapter 2:

TIME AND PLACE

Deep Time | A BRIEF HISTORY OF EARTH

The earth is 4.5 billion years old. That's a lot of time. To make the history of the earth easier to talk about, scientists divide it into smaller chunks. The largest of these time chunks is called an eon. The entire history of Earth is divided into four eons. The first eon is called the Hadean. At the beginning of the Hadean, nothing could live on Earth. It had no **atmosphere**, and its surface boiled with volcanoes. Slowly, the earth changed. Its outer surface cooled and hardened. Volcanoes released gases, including carbon dioxide. These gases began to form an atmosphere. Hot steam in the air changed to liquid water and began to pool into seas.

Then, around 4 billion years ago, the first life appeared. **Evolution** began (see page 47). During the Archean Eon, all earthly life was simple, small and slimy. Bacteria, algae

4,500 million years ago	4,000 million years ago	2,500 million years ago
HADEAN EON	ARCHEAN EON	

First simple life forms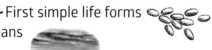

First oceans

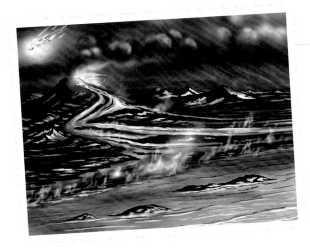

Back in the Hadean, a volcano spews smoke and a river of lava that flows to the edge of an ancient sea.

and other tiny life thrived. Throughout the next eon, the Proterozoic, this early life slowly changed the atmosphere. It took in the gas carbon dioxide and released the gas oxygen. With water, oxygen and lots of smaller life to eat, the first animals evolved around 670 million years ago.

The final eon is called the **Phanerozoic**. During this time, animals and plants similar to those of today evolved. Early plant and animal life began in the oceans but quickly spread to the land. The Phanerozoic Eon is divided into three eras: the **Paleozoic**, the **Mesozoic** and the **Cenozoic**. Plants, insects, fish, amphibians and reptiles all evolved during the Paleozoic Era. During the Mesozoic Era, **mammals** evolved alongside another major animal group: dinosaurs.

541 million years ago	0 million years ago
PROTEROZOIC EON	**PHANEROZOIC EON**

First animals

The geologic time scale divides the entire history of our planet into many smaller pieces of time.

MASTERS OF THE MESOZOIC

The Mesozoic Era lasted from 252.2 million to 65.5 million years ago. A lot happened in that time. The Mesozoic is made up of three time periods: the **Triassic**, **Jurassic** and **Cretaceous**.

During the Triassic Period, all the world's continents were stuck together. They formed a single supercontinent called Pangaea (pan-GEE-uh). Because Pangaea was so large, much of its land was a long way from the ocean. This created a lot of hot, dry environments.

The first dinosaurs were small animals, no bigger than chickens. These early dinosaurs were carnivorous, but they only ate small animals. During much of the Triassic, the scariest animals were not dinosaurs but big relatives of modern crocodiles. Early dinosaurs had to watch out for these larger predators. Luckily for dinosaurs, they were fast and could run on their long back legs. Triassic dinosaurs spread across Pangaea and evolved into many different species. As they evolved, some grew bigger.

The Jurassic Period was truly a time ruled by dinosaurs. Pangaea broke apart into smaller pieces of land. Species after species of dinosaur evolved, went extinct and were replaced by new dinosaur species. Now huge long-necked dinosaurs and armour-plated **stegosaurs** walked the earth. Ferocious

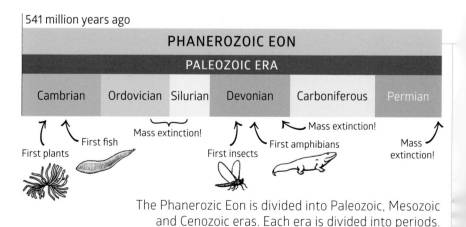

The Phanerozic Eon is divided into Paleozoic, Mesozoic and Cenozoic eras. Each era is divided into periods.

carnivorous dinosaurs, like *Allosaurus*, stood at the top of the food chain. Many new types of small dinosaurs scampered across the plains, dug burrows in the Jurassic ground and climbed in the treetops. Birds evolved.

At the end of the Jurassic, many dinosaurs went extinct. But during the Cretaceous Period, more species of dinosaurs evolved than ever before. There were duck-billed and horned dinosaurs. There were raptors and the most terrifying of all dinosaur predators: the tyrannosaurs. Then there was a sudden extinction. The Age of Dinosaurs came to a close.

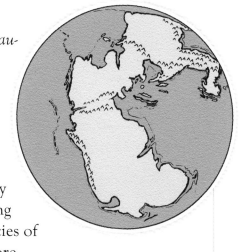

All of Earth's land was connected together 230 million years ago. This supercontinent was called Pangaea.

It is often said that dinosaurs lived a very long time ago. That is absolutely true. But you should also remember that dinosaurs lived *for* an even longer time. Late-evolving dinosaurs—like *Tyrannosaurus rex*—are separated from the first dinosaurs by more than 165 million years. That's more than twice as much time as separates *Tyrannosaurus rex*...from you and me.

252.2 million years ago		65.5 million years ago	0 million years ago
PHANEROZOIC EON			
MESOZOIC ERA			CENOZOIC ERA
Triassic	Jurassic	Cretaceous	Paleogene / Neogene / Quaternary

First dinosaurs — First mammals — Mass extinction! — First birds — Mass extinction! — First humans

"AGE OF DINOSAURS"   "AGE OF MAMMALS"

A herd of the long-necked *Apatosaurus* browses through a Jurassic savannah. With brute force, they knock down treetops that have grown too tall for them to reach. A flock of long-tailed pterosaurs, *Harpactognathus*, soars overhead.

SURVIVAL OF THE FITTEST: HOW ONE SPECIES BECOMES ANOTHER

How did one species of dinosaur, or mammal, or frog, or earthworm, or mushroom suddenly change into another species? They didn't. New species develop slowly through a process called evolution. Here's how it works:

Imagine a large group of dinosaurs of the same species. Now, just because they are all the same species does not mean they are all identical. After all, we humans are the same species, but you are not the same as everyone else. So the dinosaurs in the group all look mostly the same, but they have their differences. Let's say a few have slightly longer horns. Not a lot longer, just a little. Longer horns might help dinosaurs win fights. If so, then the dinosaurs with the longer horns will probably live longer. Living longer means having more time to find a mate and produce eggs.

You've probably been told that, in some ways, you look like your parents. Maybe someone has said: "You have your mother's eyes." Or "You've got your dad's curly hair." We often resemble our parents and share **traits** with them. The same is true for all living creatures. So the babies of the long-horned dinosaurs are likely to also have long horns. The babies with those long horns will also be better at fighting. They will probably also live longer and **produce** more eggs.

What about all the babies of the dinosaurs that did not have the long horns? Well, they were not as good at fighting and surviving. They were more likely to get eaten. In nature, survival is difficult. There is only so much food and only so much habitat. So eventually, after many generations, all the short-horned dinosaurs would die off.

Now we have a new group: all long-horned dinosaurs. Again, each dinosaur is not exactly the same. Maybe a few

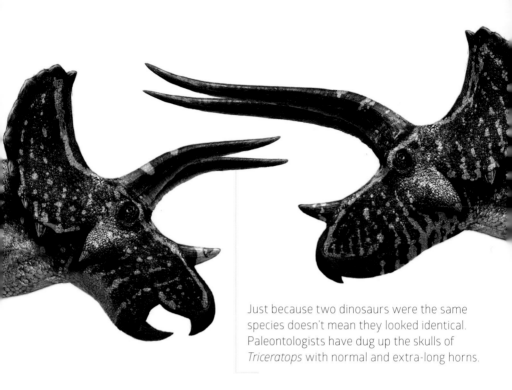

Just because two dinosaurs were the same
species doesn't mean they looked identical.
Paleontologists have dug up the skulls of
Triceratops with normal and extra-long horns.

have horns that are just a little longer still. The process
repeats. After thousands of years, and many more generations, we have a group of dinosaurs that all have horns
much longer than those of the original group. Maybe the
new group has changed in other ways too. There are many
traits that can help a dinosaur survive. Maybe some of the
dinosaurs had slightly harder skin or better camouflage or
stronger legs. All these helpful traits might mix together.
Eventually, you have a group of long-horned, hard-skinned,
better-camouflaged and stronger-legged dinosaurs. This
group is now so different from the original group that it's a
different species.

ADAPTING FOR SUCCESS

Not every new trait helped a dinosaur survive and produce
more eggs. Often, new traits were problems. Sometimes they
made dinosaurs likely to die sooner. Those longer horns

could have been a really bad thing. They could make a dinosaur's head heavier and awkward. This would make it a little harder for a dinosaur to move quickly. When thinking about evolution, we measure success by how many babies live long enough to produce babies of their own.

It is also important to remember that traits that helped make one kind of dinosaur successful might not have helped another. **Sauropodomorph** dinosaurs had long necks for reaching high into trees. These long necks made sauropodomorphs very successful in woodlands. But long necks wouldn't have helped horned dinosaurs, like *Triceratops*. Horned dinosaurs ate low-growing plants, so they didn't need to reach treetops. They did need short, strong necks to support their armoured skulls. Different kinds of dinosaurs evolved to live in different ways and in different habitats. Traits that evolved to help a species succeed in a particular way are called **adaptations**.

A *Chasmosaurus* stops for a cool drink at a river. Farther down, a *Euoplocephalus* prepares to cross the water. In the background, a herd of *Corythosaurus* passes by. In Cretaceous Alberta, all three of these big herbivores lived side by side.

Cretaceous Alberta

PALEOECOLOGY

Like all animals, every dinosaur was once a part of an eco-system. An ecosystem is a habitat and all the life within it. Even though dinosaurs were big, most of them played only a small part in their ecosystems. They were hugely outnum-bered by plants, insects, amphibians and smaller reptiles. The science of understanding extinct ecosystems is called **paleoecology**. To really understand the Late Cretaceous ecosystems of Alberta, we need to start with the smaller and more common species that grew, squirmed and scurried in the dinosaurs' shadows. This includes lily pad–like plants, clams, snails, dragonflies, fish, turtles and crocodiles.

An Albertan wetland teems with life 66 million years ago. Horns at the ready, a *Triceratops* backs away from an approaching *Tyrannosaurus*, while another *Tyrannosaurus* stalks through the trees. A white-feathered *Saurornitholestes* squabbles with the badger-sized mammal *Didelphodon* over a clam. A turtle sits happily in the water, looking to catch some tiny fish.

Unlike dinosaurs, all these smaller species have modern relatives that haven't changed much since the Cretaceous. Paleontologists can study these modern species to learn what kinds of ecosystems they belong in. All the living things just listed inhabit modern coastal wetlands. So these species show that Cretaceous Alberta was also filled with wetlands.

Cretaceous Alberta was probably a lot like the swampy habitat of modern Florida. But there were a few important differences. Many of today's animals and plants hadn't evolved yet. There were no rodents, bats or songbirds.

Walking through an Albertan swamp, the duckbill *Edmontosaurus* is one species among many. Trees, shrubs and ferns flourish in the wet and warm climate. Turtles and crocodiles relax at the edge of a pond. In the background, a large ceratopsian walks out of the forest.

Unlike any modern marsh or bayou, Cretaceous wetlands had few flowering plants. That might seem like a tiny difference, but it had a big impact on the ecosystem as a whole. With fewer flowers, there were fewer nectar-eating insects. Fewer insects meant there were also fewer insect-eating mammals, birds and reptiles.

An alligator lurks in a hot Florida swamp. Today, the wetlands of Florida are home to many of the same kinds of animals and plants that lived in Cretaceous Alberta.

TURTLE POWER

The Cretaceous was a good time to be a turtle. Turtles had already been around for many tens of millions of years. But in more ancient times, turtles were never very common. That's because they had a problem. Early turtles had large shells to protect their bodies, but they could not tuck in their heads. Instead, armoured plates covered their skulls and necks. This armour only partly protected turtles. It also restricted their necks and slowed them down. But Cretaceous turtles had evolved the ability to fully pull their heads back into the safety of their shells. This turned turtles into the walking fortresses that we know today. With this adaptation, many new turtle species evolved.

This fossilized turtle skull shows that Cretaceous turtles had large beaks and no teeth—just like the turtles of today.

This is the top of a prehistoric turtle shell. The outer part of the shell (right) is made of thick bone. On the inside (left), you can see the vertebrae and ribs that are connected to the shell.

FURRY NIGHT LIFE: MESOZOIC MAMMALS

What about our own prehistoric mammal relatives? Just like today, Cretaceous mammals had hair and drank their mother's milk as babies. Unlike today, they were all tiny. Some grew as big as opossums, but most were the size of mice and squirrels. Mammals stayed small because Cretaceous Alberta was a tough neighbourhood. Little bodies made it easier to hide from hungry dinosaurs. Many mammals were also nocturnal—meaning they were active only at night. Mammals could use their excellent sense of hearing to help find food. Under the cover of darkness, they could also avoid being seen and eaten by carnivorous dinosaurs.

CROCODILE SMILE

Look closely at the upper and lower jaws of this Cretaceous crocodile. You will notice that the teeth come in two shapes. The teeth in the front of the jaws are tall and have sharp points. These teeth are shaped for piercing soft flesh and stabbing small prey. The teeth at the back of the jaws are short, round and much less sharp. These rear teeth are good at crushing hard stuff. They allow a crocodile to crack the shells of clams and turtles, and even the thick bones of large dinosaurs. Crocodiles are predatory generalists. This means they can hunt and eat a variety of prey. This is a key to the continued success of crocodiles.

This is the skull of a Cretaceous crocodile that once swam in Alberta's wetlands.

Champsosaur skulls look a lot like crocodile skulls. But don't be fooled. Champsosaur snouts are narrower and have slender, pointy teeth.

CROC CONVERGENCE

If two species live in the same kind of habitat, eat the same kind of food and live a similar lifestyle, they will often evolve very similar adaptations. So even if the two species are not closely related to each other, they can wind up looking very similar. For example, dolphins look a lot like fish, even though they are mammals. And bats look a lot like birds. When such similarities evolve, it is called **convergent evolution**.

This skull belongs to a reptile called a champsosaur, which looked a lot like a crocodile. However, crocodiles and champsosaurs are not close relatives, even though both made a similar living as predators in shallow water. Crocodiles and champsosaurs share several traits. Both have long but thin tails, good for paddling through the water. Both have eyes and nostrils on the top of their faces. This let them breathe and see without having to expose much of their heads above the water's surface. Both have long powerful jaws, good for quickly snapping at swimming prey.

However, crocodiles and champsosaurs are far from the same. Champsosaurs have much narrower snouts and smaller teeth than most crocodiles. Champsosaurs ate only small fish, whereas Cretaceous crocodiles (like modern crocodiles) often attacked larger prey. Animals that eat only one particular kind of food are specialists. They're really good at making a living in one particular way, but if something happens to their one special food, they are in big trouble. They won't be able to eat something else.

HIGH SEAS: AN OCEAN IN ALBERTA

It's strange to think that Alberta once had beachfront property. But during much of the Age of Dinosaurs, it did. Our lost sea and shores were caused by a **greenhouse climate**. Earth once had more volcanoes than it does today. Large volcanic eruptions often filled the atmosphere with gases. Some of these gases acted like the glass walls of a greenhouse. Heat from the sun could pass through them but couldn't get out. Lots of greenhouse gases made the earth warmer than it is today. The earth was so warm there was no ice at the poles. That ice was all melted and liquid. That meant there was more water in the oceans. The extra water caused the Arctic Ocean to flood through the center of North America and create an inland sea. At its height, this seaway stretched as far south as the present Gulf of Mexico. Within this shallow sea swam sharks, sea turtles, relatives of modern squids and enormous marine reptiles.

A shark keeps its distance from a pair of mosasaurs. One of the big reptiles swims down to the sea floor and attacks an ammonite. Ammonites were relatives of squid with protective shells. All the mosasaur gets is a mouth full of ink. Yuck!

FISH LIZARDS

Ichthyosaur means "fish lizard," but **ichthyosaurs** aren't lizards, and they certainly aren't fish...nor are they dinosaurs. The name ichthyosaur still fits, though. Ichthyosaurs are a group of reptiles that looked and lived like fish. The ancestors of ichthyosaurs were reptiles who lived on land. But like the ancestors of modern sea turtles, these reptiles found success by evolving to live in the water. Ichthyosaurs had paddle-like front and hind limbs. They also evolved finned tails and shark-like dorsal fins. The long snouts of most ichthyosaurs looked like those of dolphins. Their jaws were filled with small cone-shaped teeth. This was good equipment for catching fish and other seafood. Even though ichthyosaurs had a lot in common with fish, they never evolved gills. They needed to come to the surface to fill their lungs with air.

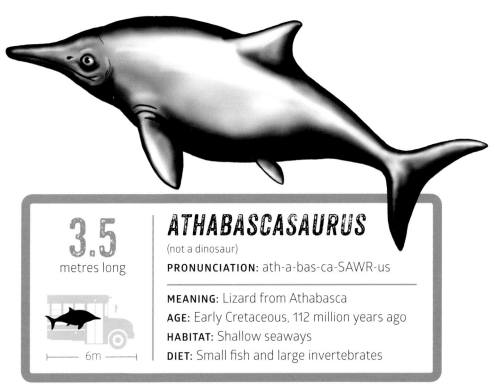

3.5
metres long

——6m——

ATHABASCASAURUS
(not a dinosaur)

PRONUNCIATION: ath-a-bas-ca-SAWR-us

MEANING: Lizard from Athabasca
AGE: Early Cretaceous, 112 million years ago
HABITAT: Shallow seaways
DIET: Small fish and large invertebrates

OCEAN MOTHER

Plesiosaurs were reptiles that swam using their enormous front flippers like underwater wings. Their hind flippers and little tail fin probably helped them steer. A plesiosaur's flippers and huge chest muscles were good for gliding through the water. But they would have been almost useless on land. Like ichthyosaurs and many other marine reptiles, plesiosaurs could not return to shore to lay eggs. Instead, they did not lay eggs at all. Mother plesiosaurs gave birth to live babies.

11

metres long

— 14m —

ALBERTONECTES

(not a dinosaur)

PRONUNCIATION: AL-ber-toh-nek-TEES

MEANING: Alberta swimmer

AGE: Late Cretaceous, 74 million years ago

HABITAT: Shallow seaways

DIET: Small fish and large invertebrates

TERRORS OF THE DEEP

Mosasaurs are another group of marine reptiles. They're closely related to today's snakes and monitor lizards (such as the Komodo dragon). Like ichthyosaurs and plesiosaurs, mosasaurs evolved paddle-like limbs to help push them through the water. Scientists once thought that mosasaurs swam by rippling their bodies and finless tails, like marine iguanas. However, research shows that mosasaurs probably held their bodies stiff while swimming. New fossil discoveries reveal they had large tail fins that could produce sudden bursts of speed. Mosasaurs had long bodies. Many species grew to more than four metres. Some mosasaurs, like *Tylosaurus*, were true sea monsters. Their bodies were longer than a school bus, and they had huge metre-long jaws. These aquatic giants were deep-sea big-game hunters. They ate large fish and other marine reptiles.

TYLOSAURUS
(not a dinosaur)

PRONUNCIATION: TY-loh-SAWR-us

MEANING: Knob lizard
AGE: Late Cretaceous, 86–75 million years ago
HABITAT: Shallow seaways
DIET: Large fish, large invertebrates, marine reptiles

13 metres long

├── 14m ──┤

Chapter 3

MEET THE FAMILY

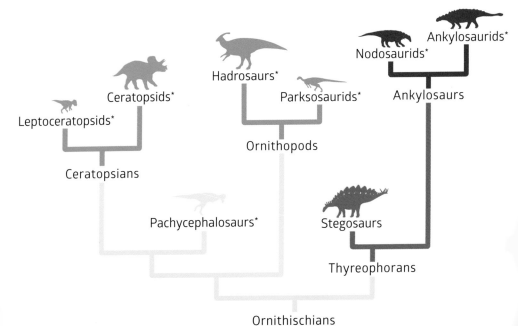

Ankylosaurids*

Nodosaurids*

Ceratopsids*

Hadrosaurs*

Parksosaurids*

Ankylosaurs

Leptoceratopsids*

Ornithopods

Ceratopsians

Pachycephalosaurs*

Stegosaurs

Thyreophorans

Ornithischians

Pterosaurs*

Crocodilians*

OTHER REPTILES

DINOSAUR DIVERSITY

Dinosaurs first evolved more than 230 million years ago. They lived on every continent, and they survived and thrived for more than 165 million years. The first dinosaurs were small two-legged carnivores. By the end of the Mesozoic, dinosaurs had evolved into all kinds of shapes and sizes. This family tree shows the major dinosaur groups and how they're related. The groups known from the Late Cretaceous of Alberta have stars after their names.

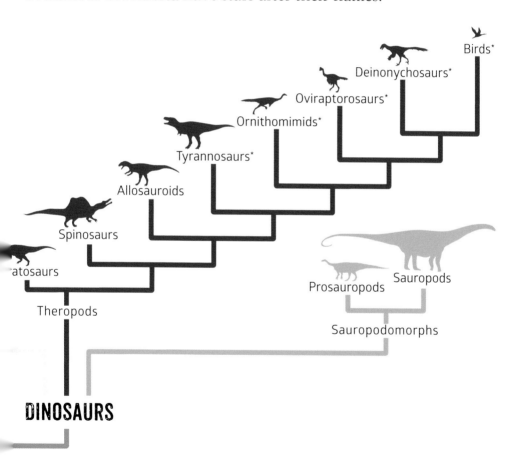

PTEROSAURS
THE FLYING REPTILES

The airways of the Age of Dinosaurs were busy places. Insects had been flying since at least as far back as 350 million years. Dinosaurs took to the air and gave rise to birds roughly 160 million years ago. There was also a third group fluttering over the heads of Alberta's dinosaurs: the pterosaurs. Pterosaurs evolved at roughly the same time that dinosaurs did (around 230 million years ago). They were the first backboned animals to fly. Pterosaur wings were very different from bird or bat wings. Birds have arms that support wings made of feathers. Bats have wings made from skin stretched between many fingers. Pterosaurs had wings of stretched skin supported by only one extremely long finger.

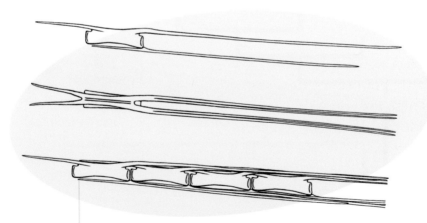

The top image shows one pterosaur tail vertebra seen from the side. The middle image shows one pterosaur tail vertebra seen from above. Notice the long rods. The bottom image shows four pterosaur tail vertebrae lined up end-to-end. You can see how the rods stack.

2.5
metre wingspan

6m

HARPACTOGNATHUS
(not a dinosaur)

PRONUNCIATION: HAR-pact-og-NAY-thuss

MEANING: Seizing jaw
AGE: Late Jurassic, 156–147 million years ago
HABITAT: Coastal shorelines
DIET: Fish

DRAGON TAILS

Early pterosaurs, like *Harpactognathus*, had long skinny tails.
These tails probably acted like rudders. They could swing
side to side to help a pterosaur turn. But long tails added
extra weight to the back end. And if the tails drooped down,
they would have disrupted the smooth flow of air over a
pterosaur's body. To fix these problems, early pterosaurs
evolved thin bony rods in the back halves of their tails.
These rods formed a brace that prevented their tails from
sagging. However, more advanced pterosaurs, like *Pter-
anodon*, did away with the problem altogether. Their tails
shrank to little stubs.

QUETZALCOATLUS
(not a dinosaur)

PRONUNCIATION: KET-zal-koh-at-lus

MEANING: Of the feathered serpent god Quetzalcoatl
AGE: Late Cretaceous, 68–66 million years ago
HABITAT: Savannahs
DIET: Unknown

11 metre wingspan

⊢——— 14m ———⊣

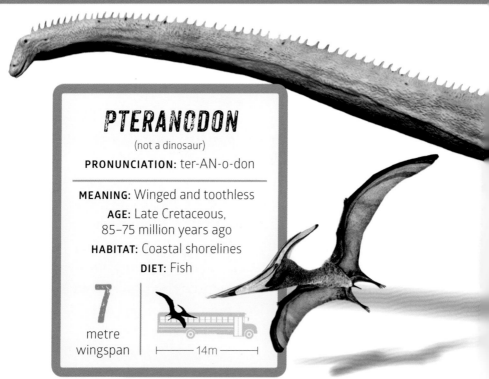

PTERANODON
(not a dinosaur)

PRONUNCIATION: ter-AN-o-don

MEANING: Winged and toothless
AGE: Late Cretaceous, 85–75 million years ago
HABITAT: Coastal shorelines
DIET: Fish

7 metre wingspan

⊢——— 14m ———⊣

SAUROPODOMORPHS
THE LONG-NECKED DINOSAURS

Sauropodomorphs were some of the first herbivorous dinosaurs. They were the biggest dinosaurs and the largest animals to ever walk the earth. Their long necks allowed them to reach high into prehistoric treetops and eat plants that were out of other dinosaurs' reach. Although their bodies were huge, sauropodomorphs had small heads. Small, light heads helped stop sauropodomorphs from hurting their long necks. But small heads meant they had small brains and small jaws. Sauropodomorphs were not as smart as many other dinosaurs, and most sauropodomorphs did not chew their food. Instead, they bit off mouthfuls of leaves and swallowed them right down.

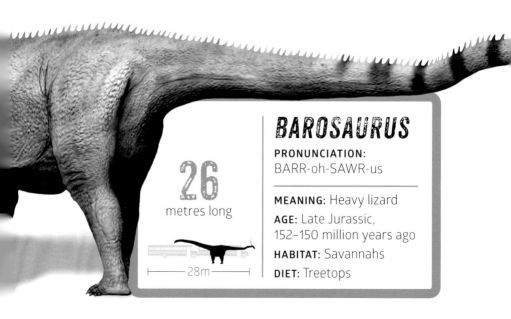

BAROSAURUS

26 metres long

28m

PRONUNCIATION: BARR-oh-SAWR-us

MEANING: Heavy lizard
AGE: Late Jurassic, 152–150 million years ago
HABITAT: Savannahs
DIET: Treetops

This nest of eggs belonged to a sauropodomorph. As big as they were as adults, *Alamosaurus* and its relatives hatched from eggs no bigger than grapefruits.

Now that's a big bone! Here I am standing next to the femur (upper leg bone) of a sauropodomorph.

LAST STAND OF THE *ALAMOSAURUS*

Back in the Jurassic, the long-necked sauropodomorphs were the main big herbivores in North America. By the Late Cretaceous, that had changed. Although there were still many sauropodomorphs living on other continents, in North America, most sauropodomorphs had become extinct. Smaller herbivores, like ceratopsians and hadrosaurs, took over. But there were a few big exceptions. The rare and huge *Alamosaurus* was one of North America's last sauropodomorphs. *Alamosaurus* survived until the very end of the Age of Dinosaurs.

ALAMOSAURUS

PRONUNCIATION:
AL-uh-mo-SAWR-us

MEANING: Lizard from the Ojo Alamo Formation

AGE: Late Cretaceous, 70–66 million years ago

HABITAT: Savannahs

DIET: Treetops

30 metres long

←28m→

THEROPODS

THE SHARP-TOOTHED DINOSAURS

The **theropods** include all the carnivorous dinosaurs, like the famous *Tyrannosaurus* and *Velociraptor*. These dinosaurs had hooked claws and pointed teeth. The theropods also include some herbivorous dinosaurs that evolved from carnivorous ancestors. Birds are in the theropod branch of the dinosaur family tree. This makes theropods the longest-lived and most diverse of all dinosaur groups.

10
metres long

— 14m —

GORGOSAURUS

PRONUNCIATION: gor-GO-SAWR-us

MEANING: Fierce lizard
AGE: Late Cretaceous, 76–75 million years ago
HABITAT: Flood plains and wetlands
DIET: Other dinosaurs

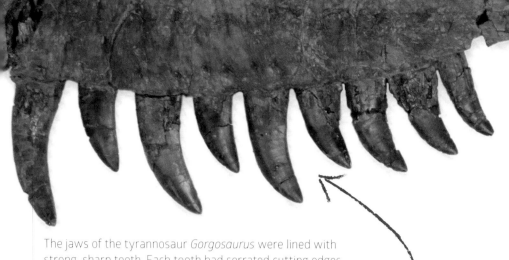

The jaws of the tyrannosaur *Gorgosaurus* were lined with strong, sharp teeth. Each tooth had serrated cutting edges.

ON THE CUTTING EDGE

These are the teeth of the tyrannosaur *Gorgosaurus*. Look closely and you'll see each tooth's cutting edges. Notice that the edges are lined with small bumps. These bumps form a serrated edge. Like the serrated edge on a saw, it helps the tooth to cut. The teeth of most predatory dinosaurs had two serrated edges, one on the front and one on the back. Serrated edges helped teeth pierce flesh during a bite. They also helped tear flesh as the predator tugged backwards.

COLUMBA
(pigeon)

PRONUNCIATION: CO-lum-ba

0.7 metre wingspan ├───── 6m ─────┤

MEANING: Diver

AGE: Neogene, 8–0 million years ago

HABITAT: Woodlands, grasslands, semi-deserts, urban areas

DIET: Seeds, insects and breadcrumbs

Paleontologists uncover the killing claw of the raptor *Saurornitholestes* in the field.

RAPTOR CLAWS

Saurornitholestes and *Troodon* are **deinonychosaurs.** Deinonychosaurs are a group of theropods better known as raptors. Compared to other types of carnivorous dinosaurs, deinonychosaurs had weak jaws and small teeth. Instead, their primary killing tools were toenails. On each foot, one claw was enlarged and strongly curved. These hooked claws were held up as the deinonychosaur walked and ran. This kept the claw from being dulled by the ground. Deinonychosaurs attacked prey like Cretaceous kick-boxers. They lashed out with their feet and slashed with their sharp hooked claws. Some paleontologists think deinonychosaur foot claws may have helped in another way. The claws may have been useful in tree climbing, acting like the spiked boots of a lumberjack.

The large foot claws of raptors, like this *Troodon* claw, were strongly curved and had sharp tips.

SAURORNITHOLESTES

PRONUNCIATION: SAWR-or-NITH-uh-les-teez

MEANING: Lizard-bird thief
AGE: Late Cretaceous, 77–69 million years ago
HABITAT: Wetlands
DIET: Mammals, reptiles and small dinosaurs

2 metres long

6m

TROODON

PRONUNCIATION: TROH-eh-don

MEANING: Wounding tooth
AGE: Late Cretaceous,
77–66 million years ago
HABITAT: Flood plains, wetlands
and forests
DIET: Mammals, reptiles and
small dinosaurs

2.5 metres long

6m

APEX PREDATOR

Imagine yourself as a lone adult *Gorgosaurus* in
the coastal marshes of Cretaceous Alberta. Your
head towers four metres in the air. You're standing
by the body of a young *Centrosaurus* that you have just
killed with a single bite from your monstrous jaws. Still,
you're nervous. Your keen eyes scan the edge of a swampy
forest. Your keener nose sniffs the air. You smell something...something dangerous. The smell is getting stronger.
You panic, rip off a limb from the *Centrosaurus* and swallow
it as fast as you can. There is no time to eat any more! You
turn and trot away from the smell, just as the danger walks
out of the forest and sees your kill.

What could terrify a big tyrannosaur? A bigger tyrannosaur. Seventy-five million years ago, there was more than
one kind of tyrannosaur living in the wetlands and flood
plains of Alberta. The biggest of them all was *Daspletosaurus*.
Daspletosaurus might have been a direct ancestor of *Tyrannosaurus rex.*

DASPLETOSAURUS

PRONUNCIATION:
da-SPLEET-oh-SAWR-us

MEANING: Frightful lizard

AGE: Late Cretaceous,
77–74 million years ago

HABITAT: Flood plains and wetlands

DIET: Other dinosaurs

12
metres
long

14m

THE ROYAL FAMILY

The best known of all meat-eating dinosaurs is *Tyrannosaurus rex*. Its name means "tyrant lizard king." However, *T. rex* was just one species of tyrannosaur. The tyrannosaur family evolved near the end of the Age of Dinosaurs. Their fossils have been found throughout North America, Europe and Asia. Before the evolution of tyrannosaurs, other large carnivorous dinosaurs were the top predators. Tyrannosaurs did not evolve from any of these other large predators. They did not inherit their position as "tyrant kings" from their ancestors. Instead, tyrannosaurs took over. As tyrannosaurs got bigger, they began to eat the same prey as other kinds

TYRANNOSAURUS

PRONUNCIATION:
TY-RAN-oh-SAWR-us

MEANING: Tyrant lizard
AGE: Late Cretaceous,
67–66 million years ago
HABITAT: Flood plains and wetlands
DIET: Other dinosaurs

12 metres long

├─── 14m ───┤

of large carnivorous dinosaurs. These other large carnivores couldn't handle the new competition. Eventually, they went extinct. Only the tyrannosaurs remained.

They're not fighting…that's a love bite. It's hard to know what dinosaur courtship was like. Here, artist Dr. Julius Csotonyi has speculated that mating tyrannosaurs lightly nipped their partners on the back of the head. Many birds and big cats do the same.

DISARMED AND DANGEROUS

Tyrannosaurs are famous for having arms that are tiny compared to their great body size. Compare these two arms. One belongs to the 9-metre-long carnivorous dinosaur *Allosaurus* (not a tyrannosaur). The other belongs to a 12-metre-long *Tyrannosaurus*. You can see that the *Allosaurus* arm has three fingers and the *Tyrannosaurus* has two. The *Allosaurus* is a smaller dinosaur, but its arm is much longer. The *Tyrannosaurus* arm is shorter, and each arm bone is also much skinnier. Look closely and you'll see that the bones in both arms have ridges or crests. These crests are where arm and chest muscles attach. The bigger the crest, the bigger and stronger the muscle that attached to it. The *Tyrannosaurus* arm bones have crests that are much shorter. This means that tyrannosaur arms were weak compared to other dinosaurs' arms. However, the ancestors of tyrannosaurs had normal-sized and -muscled forelimbs with three fingers. Why would tyrannosaurs have evolved short arms with weaker muscles and one less finger? How did that help them survive? The answer: teeth and balance.

Tyrannosaurus

Small crests for muscle attachments

Allosaurus

Big crests for muscle attachments

Compare the size of the muscle-attachment crests on the arms of *Tyrannosaurus* and *Allosaurus*. Although tyrannosaur arms were much stronger than any human's, they were weak compared to most other big carnivorous dinosaurs.

ALLOSAURUS

PRONUNCIATION: AL-oh-SAWR-us

MEANING: Different lizard
AGE: Late Jurassic, 156–145 million years ago
HABITAT: Savannahs
DIET: Other dinosaurs

9 metres long

├─── 14m ───┤

JAWBREAKERS

Here's another comparison. Look at this tooth from the carnivorous dinosaur *Acrocanthosaurus* (a relative of *Allosaurus*) and this tooth from *Tyrannosaurus*. The *Acrocanthosaurus* fang has a sharp point and a flattened knifelike shape. This is normal for carnivorous dinosaur teeth. But the *Tyrannosaurus* tooth is different. It has a blunt tip and is thick. These differences give the tyrannosaur tooth the potential to do more than simply slice through soft flesh. Tyrannosaur teeth can crush bones.

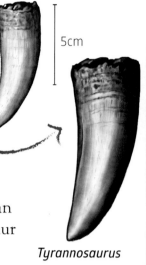

Acrocanthosaurus

5cm

Tyrannosaurus

TOOTH AND CONSEQUENCES

When biting down hard on solid bone, most carnivorous dinosaur teeth would have been in danger of snapping. But tyrannosaur teeth were strong enough to punch right through. Bone-shattering teeth could deal serious wounds. However, they came with a cost. These teeth only worked properly with the help of enormous jaw muscles. Such hugely muscled jaws would have made tyrannosaurs top heavy. Carnivorous dinosaurs were built like see-saws. They stood on only their hind legs and held their bodies mostly flat. On the back half of a tyrannosaur see-saw was the long heavy tail.

The tyrannosaur *Daspletosaurus* had large and powerful jaws. The jaw bones of tyrannosaurs were much thicker than those of other carnivorous dinosaurs.

ACROCANTHOSAURUS

PRONUNCIATION: ACK-roe-CANTH-oh-SAWR-us

MEANING: High-spined lizard
AGE: Early Cretaceous, 116–110 million years ago
HABITAT: Savannahs
DIET: Other dinosaurs

11
metres long

⊢————— 14m —————⊣

Even the thick leg bones of hadrosaurs and ceratopsians were no match for the biting power of big tyrannosaurs. A tyrannosaur tooth stabbed right through this bone and made the large hole.

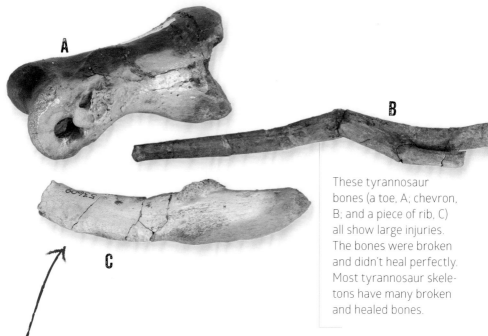

These tyrannosaur bones (a toe, A; chevron, B; and a piece of rib, C) all show large injuries. The bones were broken and didn't heal perfectly. Most tyrannosaur skeletons have many broken and healed bones.

On the front half was the torso, arms, neck and head. Growing big jaw muscles would have added weight to the front half. So unless tyrannosaurs lost weight from somewhere else on their front end or grew ridiculously long tails, their see-saw bodies would have been out of balance. They would have fallen flat on their faces.

The evolutionary solution was to shrink the arms. This reduced weight in the front and allowed tyrannosaurs to bulk up their biting power. Tyrannosaur ancestors were three fingered, long armed, weak jawed and thin toothed. Gradually, the arms shrank, the jaws strengthened and the teeth swelled. Eventually, species like *Tyrannosaurus rex* evolved.

IT'S HARD TO BE THE KING

All of these tyrannosaur bones are **pathologic**. This means their shapes have been damaged by injury or infection. Although being the "king of the dinosaurs" may sound glamorous, tyrannosaurs had it rough. They hunted horned ceratopsians and **ankylosaurs** with tail clubs. It was a hard-knock life. Almost every tyrannosaur skeleton ever unearthed has lots of large injuries.

LITTLE TERROR

Nanotyrannus is a small tyrannosaur that lived alongside the giant *Tyrannosaurus*. Paleontologists have been arguing about it since it was discovered in 1988. Is it a baby *Tyrannosaurus* or a completely different kind of dinosaur? No one knows for sure. But new research indicates that the leg bones of *Nanotyrannus* were longer than the leg bones of *Tyrannosaurus* juveniles. How could *Nanotyrannus* and *Tyrannosaurus* live together in the same ecosystem? Maybe, like modern lions and cheetahs, one was adapted to attack very big game. And the other, with its longer legs, was adapted to chase down smaller and faster prey.

NANOTYRANNUS

PRONUNCIATION: NA-no-TY-RAN-us

MEANING: Tiny tyrant
AGE: Late Cretaceous, 67–66 million years ago
HABITAT: Flood plains and wetlands
DIET: Small and medium dinosaurs

6 metres long

├───── 14m ─────┤

ETIQUETTE REX

When all the chasing and killing was done, it was time for a well-earned meal. With such little arms, you might think that tyrannosaur feeding had all the gory awkwardness of a no-hands pie-eating contest. However, for any big predator, meals are hard to come by. An animal can't afford to waste bits of hard-won meat because of bad table manners.

Paleontologists have studied where muscles attach to the neck bones of tyrannosaurs. Tyrannosaur necks were good for lunging forward at prey and pulling backwards to rip off mouthfuls of flesh. They were also shaped to help tyrannosaurs eat without making a mess. A tyrannosaur's neck muscles allowed it to bite and then twist its head powerfully to the side. This would be very useful for yanking off limbs. A dining tyrannosaur could have turned a single dead dinosaur into five or six smaller pieces. Then a bite and quick upwards flip of the neck would have swung one of those pieces into the air. A tyrannosaur could open its mouth and gravity would have helped it swallow the whole piece in one big gulp. This is the same way that modern crocodiles and birds of prey feed. No chewing or hands required.

To eat like a *T. rex*, first you grab and rip off a mouthful of *Triceratops*. Then you flip your head upwards and gulp it down—bones and all!

Dr. Angelica Torices
Telling Teeth

These three teeth were all found in the Late Cretaceous badlands of Alberta. Each is from a different kind of tyrannosaur. Can you tell what kind each tooth came from? Neither can most paleontologists.

Throughout its life, a tyrannosaur was constantly growing and shedding teeth. Teeth are partly made of **enamel**. Enamel is even harder and stronger than bone. So tyrannosaur teeth are common dinosaur fossils to find. But if it's not possible to identify what kind of tyrannosaur the teeth came from, then they aren't very useful fossils.

Luckily, dinosaur tooth expert Dr. Angelica Torices has solved the problem. She carefully studied tyrannosaur tooth shape. She measured and counted the tooth **denticles** (the individual bumps that make up the serrated edges). She discovered that the teeth of all three common Albertan tyrannosaurs are just a little bit different. But the differences are too small to notice without measuring tools and calculations. Thanks to her research, we can identify these teeth (from top to bottom) as those of an *Albertosaurus*, a *Daspletosaurus* and a *Gorgosaurus*.

These are all tyrannosaur teeth, but they come from three different species.

THYREOPHORANS
THE ARMOURED DINOSAURS

Thyreophorans means "shield bearers." These herbivorous dinosaurs had hard, sharp, bony coverings that protected them from predators. The stegosaurs and ankylosaurs are both types of thyreophorans. Stegosaurs had spearhead-shaped armoured plates lining their backs. They also had several long spikes near the tips of their tails. Ankylosaurs had backs and tails covered in short spikes, and thick armoured skulls.

STEGOSAURUS
PRONUNCIATION: STEG-uh-SAWR-us

MEANING: Roofed lizard
AGE: Late Jurassic, 155–150 million years ago
HABITAT: Forests and wooded flood plains
DIET: Plants

9 metres long

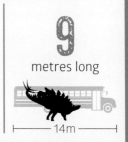

⊢————— 14m —————⊣

Dr. Victoria Arbour
War Clubs

Dr. Victoria Arbour has thought a lot about the back ends of ankylosaurs. Her research has helped us understand what may be the most dangerous tails in prehistory. Some ankylosaur species grew large pieces of armour at the end of their tails. To support this armour, the vertebrae in the back half of the tail were tightly connected. Together, the armoured tip and connected vertebrae are called the ankylosaur tail club. Dr. Arbour's research shows that these tail clubs could hit hard. Stout tail muscles were anchored to the wide hips of ankylosaurs. These supplied the tails with enough smashing power to break a tyrannosaur's leg. Ankylosaurs might have also used their tail clubs to combat other ankylosaurs. Like the tusks of elephants or the horns of buffalo, tail clubs may have been used in fights over territory or mates.

The tip of a tail club from *Euoplocephalus* is made of large strong osteoderms.

ANKYLOSAURUS

PRONUNCIATION:
AN-ky-low-SAWR-us

MEANING: Fused lizard
AGE: Late Cretaceous,
66 million years ago
HABITAT: Coastal flood plains
DIET: Low-growing plants

9 metres long

|— 14m —|

DERMAL DEFENDERS

Osteoderms are bones that grow within an animal's skin. Today, osteoderms can be found in the tough hides of crocodiles and the shells of armadillos. Many dinosaur groups also had osteoderms. They helped guard against the claws and teeth of predators. The giant arrowhead-shaped back plates of stegosaurs are one of the most spectacular examples. However, the fanciest coats of osteoderm armour belonged to the ankylosaurs. The armoured skin of ankylosaurs included osteoderm horns, spikes, plates and tail maces. Some even had thick bony eyelids.

The heads, backs and tails of ankylosaurs were covered in large bony plates. Many of the plates had sharp peaks or ridges.

A LOT OF GUTS

It's much harder to digest plants than meat. To deal with the challenge of vegetarianism, many herbivores evolved large grinding teeth and strong chewing muscles. Ankylosaurs tried something else. They kept their teeth small and their jaws weak. But they enlarged their digestive organs. With a big stomach and supersized intestines, the ribcages of ankylosaurs bulged out to the sides. They looked like barrels. This extra girth made ankylosaurs slower. But with their armoured covering, ankylosaurs didn't need to be fast or agile.

EUOPLOCEPHALUS

PRONUNCIATION: YOU-oh-plo-SEFF-ah-luss

MEANING: Well-armoured head
AGE: Late Cretaceous, 76–75 million years ago
HABITAT: Flood plains and coastal marshes
DIET: Low-growing plants

6
metres long

├── 14m ──┤

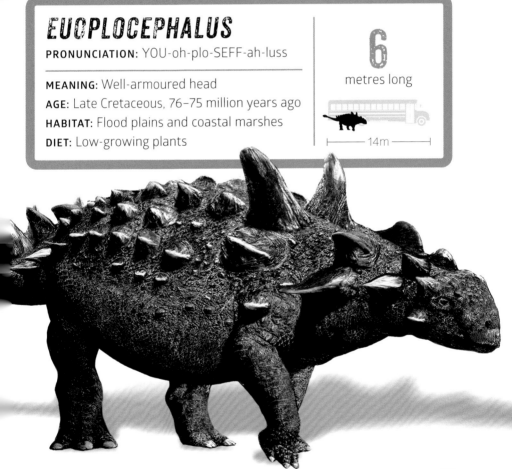

This is the half ring of the ankylosaur *Euoploceph-alus*. Half rings covered and protected the neck. Notice that the armour has four spikes.

STUDDED COLLARS

Some ankylosaurs had a pair of crescent-shaped bony plates, called **half rings**, that covered and protected their necks. Although these half rings were made of thick bone, a hungry tyrannosaur had enough biting power to easily snap them in two. But that didn't matter. Each half ring had a covering of cone-shaped osteoderms. These osteoderms were sharp and spiky. A tyrannosaur had the jaw strength to crush a half ring, but if it tried, it would have cut its own mouth.

SHOULDER PADS

There are two major families of ankylosaurs: the **ankylosaurids** and the **nodosaurids**. Ankylosaurids—like *Euoplocephalus*—have tail clubs and backwards-pointing horns on their heads. Nodosaurids—like *Edmontonia*—usually don't have horns or tail clubs. Instead, some nodosaurids evolved large spikes over their shoulders. When threatened, these nodosaurids probably charged forward and tried to shoulder check their enemies.

EDMONTONIA

PRONUNCIATION: ED-mon-TONE-ee-ah

MEANING: From the Edmonton Formation
AGE: Late Cretaceous, 76–71 million years ago
HABITAT: Wetlands
DIET: Plants

6.5
metres long

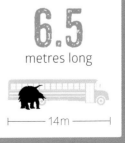

├── 14m ──┤

PICKY EATERS

Look at these skulls. You can see another important difference between nodosaurids and ankylosaurids. Nodosaurids had narrow snouts with small beaks. Ankylosaurids had short rounded snouts with broad beaks. Although these two armoured herbivores lived side by side, they had very different eating habits. With their short broad beaks, ankylosaurids could scarf down big mouthfuls of plants. Nodosaurids went for quality over quantity. They used their smaller and narrower beaks to snip off only the juiciest leaves and stems.

Horn

Horn

This is the skull of the ankylosaurid *Euoplocephalus*. Notice the horns at the back of the skull and the short wide snout.

This is the skull of the nodosaurid *Edmontonia*. Notice the long snout.

SNORTING A SYMPHONY

Big osteoderm spikes were not the only kind of horns ankylosaurs carried. The armoured dinosaurs also had musical horns in their noses. Paleontologists X-rayed ankylosaur skulls. They discovered that the dinosaurs' nostrils lead to looping hollow tunnels. Like the tubular body of a trumpet or French horn, these tunnels may have amplified sound as air travelled through them. Bellowing through its nose, an ankylosaur could have produced a honking-loud sound. The pattern of tunnel loops is different for every ankylosaur species. Like modern songbirds, no ankylosaur species had the same call.

Inside the skull of *Euoplocephalus*, looping air tunnels turned the nose into a musical instrument.

PACHYCEPHALOSAURS
THE DOME-HEADED DINOSAURS

Pachycephalosaurs are an uncommon group of dinosaurs. Some were as big as horses. But most were as small as dogs. All of them walked on their back legs and had small arms, barrel-shaped bodies and tails stiffened by extra bones. Many also had domed skulls with lots of small horns. Pachycephalosaurs were mostly plant eaters, though they had sharp canine-like teeth at the front of their jaws. They may have used these teeth to occasionally eat meat.

PACHYCEPHALOSAURUS
PRONUNCIATION: pac-KEY-sef-a-lo-SAWR-us

MEANING: Thick-headed lizard
AGE: Late Cretaceous, 70–66 million years ago
HABITAT: Flood plains
DIET: Plants (possibly some small animals)

4.5 metres long

|— 14m —|

SKULL CAPS

The fossils of pachycephalosaurs are extremely rare...except for the skull domes. The domes are several inches thick and made of solid bone. Predators and scavengers weren't interested in eating them. The same toughness that made pachycephalosaur domes good at absorbing head-butt impact also made them durable fossils. Museums often have drawers filled with pachycephalosaur skull domes but no skeletons.

These lumpy fossils are all skull caps from pachycephalosaurs. They were each found by themselves, with no other bones nearby.

The skull of the pachycephalosaur *Stegoceras* is topped with a thick dome of bone.

Dr. Eric Snively
Crash Test

Most pachycephalosaurs had thick bony domes on top of their heads. Paleontologists have always thought the domes might have been natural helmets. Maybe they allowed the dinosaurs to bash headlong into predators. Or to ram head-to-head with other pachyceph-alosaurs in butting competitions. But without living pachycephalosaurs, how could this head-butting idea be tested?

Dr. Eric Snively seems to have found a way. Dr. Snively X-rayed the skulls of many modern animals, including those that often butt heads, like muskoxen. This showed Dr. Snively what the inside of the different skulls looked like. He then created 3-D models of the skulls using a computer. Dr. Snively experimented with the 3-D models using what's called finite element analyses (or FEA for short). FEA computer experiments are used to calculate the strength of things like bridges, buildings or new machines. They calculate what parts of an object are the weakest and how much force is needed to break them.

The FEA experiments showed that modern animals that do not usually butt heads have skulls that break under strong force. However, the skulls of head-butting animals can easily withstand strong force. This skull strength comes from special internal bone structures. These are adaptations that head-butters have evolved to absorb extra stress.

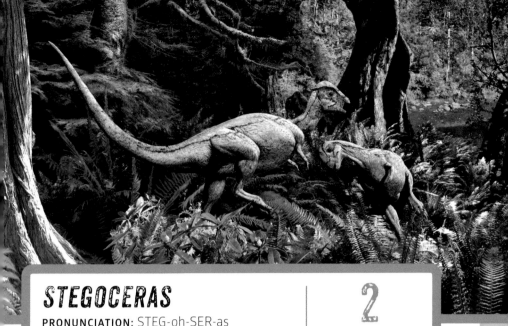

STEGOCERAS

PRONUNCIATION: STEG-oh-SER-as

MEANING: Roof horned
AGE: Late Cretaceous, 77–74 million years ago
HABITAT: Wetlands
DIET: Plants (possibly some small animals)

2 metres long

⊢ 6m ⊣

Next, Dr. Snively tried the FEA experiments on a skull of the pachy-cephalosaur *Stegoceras*. He learned that the *Stegoceras* skull was also strong enough to survive head-on collisions. Even without a live pachycephalosaur to test, Dr. Snively solved the mystery.

This is a computer model of a *Stegoceras* skull. Dr. Snively used it to figure out if pachycephalosaur domes were strong enough to survive head-butting. The dark blue is bone. The other colours show what happens during a head-butt. When a strong force (red colours) hits the thick dome, the force is quickly absorbed and becomes weak and harmless (green colours). *Eric Snively image*

CERATOPSIANS
THE HORNED DINOSAURS

The ceratopsians were another herbivorous group that evolved late in the history of dinosaurs. They had very strong jaws, with hooked parrot-like beaks and rows of teeth in the rear. Most ceratopsian heads also had large horns and a shield of bone on the back of the skulls. These shields protected the neck. Often, the shields were lined with small horns.

UNESCOCERATOPS

PRONUNCIATION: YU-nes-co-SEH-rah-tops

MEANING: UNESCO (United Nations Educational, Scientific and Cultural Organization) horned face
AGE: Late Cretaceous, 76–75 million years ago
HABITAT: Wetlands
DIET: Plants

2 metres long

6m

TRICERATOPS

PRONUNCIATION: TRY-SEH-rah-tops

MEANING: Three-horned face
AGE: Late Cretaceous, 68–66 million years ago
HABITAT: Wetlands
DIET: Plants

8 metres long

14m

SPEAR HEAD

Styracosaurus had an impressive head. It was armed with a single tall horn on its snout and a fan of tall horns on its neck shield. *Styracosaurus* probably also had another, less obvious, weapon: cooperation. The skeletons of multiple *Styracosaurus* have been found buried together in a single large bonebed. Because so many *Styracosaurus* died together, they were probably all living together in one large herd. A lone charging *Styracosaurus* would have threatened even the hungriest tyrannosaur. A stampeding *Styracosaurus* herd would have been a living avalanche!

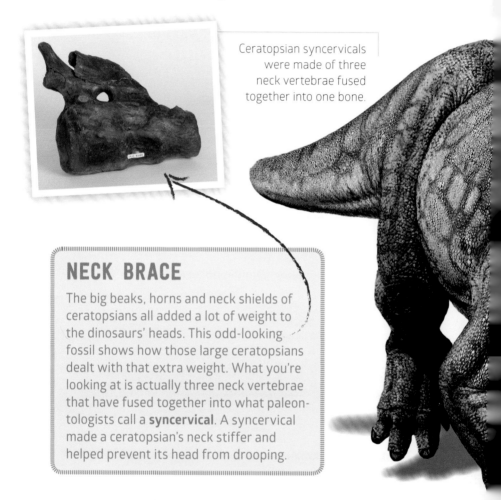

Ceratopsian syncervicals were made of three neck vertebrae fused together into one bone.

NECK BRACE

The big beaks, horns and neck shields of ceratopsians all added a lot of weight to the dinosaurs' heads. This odd-looking fossil shows how those large ceratopsians dealt with that extra weight. What you're looking at is actually three neck vertebrae that have fused together into what paleontologists call a **syncervical**. A syncervical made a ceratopsian's neck stiffer and helped prevent its head from drooping.

STYRACOSAURUS

PRONUNCIATION:
STY-rack-o-SAWR-us

MEANING: Spiked lizard
AGE: Late Cretaceous,
75 million years ago
HABITAT: Wetlands
DIET: Plants

5 metres long

6m

BLOOD LINES

The horns of modern animals, like antelope, bison and cattle, are made of more than bone. Bone forms only the inside, or core, of a horn. There's an outer covering too. It's made of a material called **keratin**—the same thing as your fingernails. Keratin is tough stuff. It can bend without breaking, can be very sharp and grows quickly. Look at this *Centrosaurus* snout horn. You'll notice it has lots of grooves across its surface. These grooves are blood channels. The bony horn-cores of many modern animals are also covered in blood channels. These blood channels supply oxygen and nutrients to help the keratin covering grow. So even though keratin doesn't normally fossilize, we know dinosaur horns were covered with it. In modern animals, the keratin covering is often much longer than the bony horn-core beneath it, and the keratin is much sharper. The horns of dinosaurs were probably also longer and sharper than can be judged from only their horn-cores.

On this ceratopsian nose horn you can see many small grooves. These grooves are where blood once flowed across the horn.

The horns of this modern cow skull are made of a bony core and a covering of keratin. The horn cores have holes and channels where blood flows to the keratin.

CENTROSAURUS

PRONUNCIATION: SEN-tro-SAWR-us

MEANING: Pointed lizard
AGE: Late Cretaceous, 77–76 million years ago
HABITAT: Wetlands
DIET: Plants

6 metres long

14m

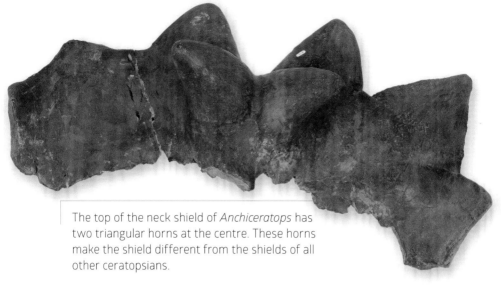

The top of the neck shield of *Anchiceratops* has two triangular horns at the centre. These horns make the shield different from the shields of all other ceratopsians.

FRILL FUNCTION AND FASHION

Ceratopsian neck shields probably had many jobs. The shields were usually lined with bony spikes. These would cut into any predator that tried to attack the ceratopsian's neck. Often, the shields had extra spikes or ridges. Some of them stuck out or curled in a way that doesn't seem useful as protection. Scientists think these decorative parts helped dinosaurs attract mates, like the crests of birds and antlers of deer.

Each ceratopsian species has its own pattern of shield ornaments. The pair of forward-pointing triangular horns on the centre of this shield is only found in *Anchiceratops*. Some scientists think the shields were also natural ID badges. They might have helped a ceratopsian quickly recognize members of its own species.

MUCKING ABOUT

For large animals, life in a wetland can be a sticky situation. Ceratopsians weighed several tons. Their feet would have been in danger of sinking deep into the muddy ground. A stuck dinosaur couldn't get away from predators and might even have become permanently trapped. One way to deal with soggy ground is to have big feet with wide-spreading toes, like a hippopotamus. Ceratopsians had exactly that kind of feet. Big feet helped to spread out their weight and stopped the dinosaurs from getting bogged down.

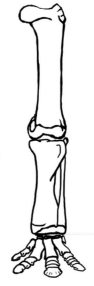

The back leg of *Triceratops* had four wide spreading toes, just like a modern hippopotamus.

ANCHICERATOPS

PRONUNCIATION: ANG-key-SEH-rah-tops

MEANING: Near horned-face
AGE: Late Cretaceous, 72–71 million years ago
HABITAT: Wetlands
DIET: Plants

5
metres long

6m

A FACE A MOTHER COULD LOVE

Sometimes, big dinosaur discoveries come in small packages. This is the fossil skeleton of most of a baby *Chasmosaurus*. The front limbs are missing. They eroded away sometime over the last few hundred years. But the specimen is otherwise beautifully preserved. Look closely. You can see fossilized **tendons** criss-crossing its spine. Tendons are tough connecting bands that hold bones and muscles together. You can also see the faint scaly outlines of fossil skin on its side.

This fossil tells us a lot about ceratopsian **ontogeny**. Ontogeny is the study of how animals change as they grow up. Scientists compared this skeleton to skeletons of adult ceratopsians. They found out that growing up meant more changes than just getting bigger. Most baby animals have eyes that are larger compared to their heads than the eyes of adults. This baby ceratopsian has big eyes too. Another ontogenetic difference is the size of the horns. Look above each eye socket. The baby's horns are just small stubs. They wouldn't have been very useful as protection. How did this little dinosaur avoid being eaten by predators? The answer: family. This baby's skeleton was found by itself, but other baby ceratopsian skeletons have been found beside the bones of adults. This shows that ceratopsians lived in family groups. Baby horned dinosaurs did not grow their weapons until they were big enough to use them. While they were young, their fully horned parents protected them.

CHASMOSAURUS

PRONUNCIATION:
KAZ-mo-SAWR-us

MEANING: Chasm lizard

AGE: Late Cretaceous,
77–75 million years ago

HABITAT: Wetlands

DIET: Plants

5
metres
long

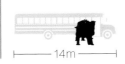

├── 14m ──┤

Look closely. You can see
fossil skin over the ribs.

This nearly complete skeleton
of a baby *Chasmosaurus*
is about the size of a
sheep. Only the front
legs are missing.

ORNITHOPODS

THE BIRD-FOOTED, PLANT-EATING DINOSAURS

Ornithopods have been called the cows and gazelles of the dinosaur world. They were some of the most common herbivores. Some ornithopods were sheep-sized grazers. Others, like the hadrosaurs, or duck-billed dinosaurs, were multi-ton giants. Small ornithopods stood on only their hind legs. Larger ornithopods usually stood on all fours, but reared back onto only their longer hind legs when running.

THE MIGHTY DUCKBILLS

What kind of dinosaur was most common throughout the forests, flood plains and marshes of Cretaceous Alberta? The hadrosaurs. The average adult hadrosaur was more than 9 metres long and weighed more than 2 metric tons.

SAUROLOPHUS

PRONUNCIATION: SAWR-OL-o-fus

MEANING: Lizard crest
AGE: Late Cretaceous, 70–68 million years ago
HABITAT: Flood plains and coastal marshes
DIET: Plants

10 metres long

— 14m —

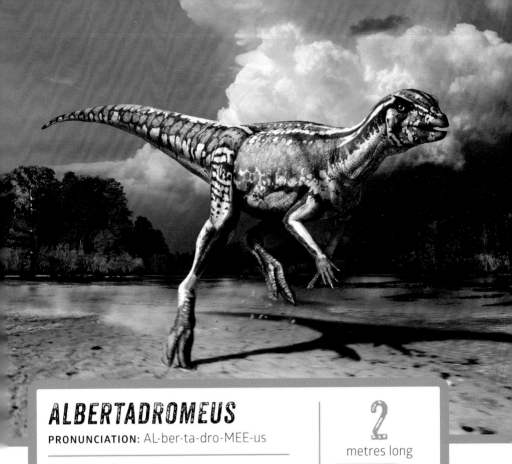

ALBERTADROMEUS

PRONUNCIATION: AL-ber-ta-dro-MEE-us

MEANING: Alberta runner
AGE: Late Cretaceous, 78–76 million years ago
HABITAT: Flood plains
DIET: Plants

2 metres long

⊢———— 6m ————⊣

Very large hadrosaurs topped the scales at more than 12 metric tons and were 12 metres from head to tail. The long snouts and broad beaks of hadrosaurs have given the group its common nickname: the duckbills. Hadrosaur faces do look like mallards', but a hadrosaur "bill" is different from a duck's in many ways. First, ducks are toothless. Hadrosaurs had rows of grinding teeth in the back of their mouths. Second, the edges of a hadrosaur beak were sharp, not smooth. Sharp is better for pruning plants.

A mother's work is never done. Once hatched, baby duck-bills didn't just leave the nest. They stayed and were brought food by their moms.

SMALL STARTS

Large modern herbivores—like elephants—usually give birth to big babies. But dinosaurs hatched from eggs. Even giant dinosaur species began life on a small scale. As a hatchling, a baby hadrosaur would have been less than half a metre long. At such sizes, hadrosaurs were vulnerable to lots of predators, but baby duckbills grew fast. They tripled in size within their first year. This fast growth continued for their first 10 years. Hadrosaurs reached their mature multi-ton mass before they were even teenagers.

PARASAUROLOPHUS
PRONUNCIATION: PAIR-a-SAWR-OL-o-fus

MEANING: Near *Saurolophus*
AGE: Late Cretaceous, 76–75 million years ago
HABITAT: Flood plains and coastal marshes
DIET: Plants

9.5 metres long

14m

Dr. Michael Burns
Knowing a Bone Inside Out

Sometimes, to learn about a dinosaur bone, you have to cut it open. Dr. Michael Burns is an expert fossil bone butcher. He uses a high-powered rock saw to slice off very thin sections of fossils. He looks at the inside of the fossils under a microscope to study how dinosaurs grew.

Just like today, the climate of Cretaceous Alberta was seasonal. During the warm and wet seasons, there was lots of food. Dinosaurs had the fuel they needed to grow quickly. During the cooler and drier seasons, there was less food. Dinosaurs grew more slowly. Like the rings of a tree trunk, a dinosaur bone records these differences in growth. Thin dense layers of bone show seasons of slow growth. Thick spongy layers of bone record seasons of fast growth. By measuring and counting these layers, Dr. Burns learns how old a dinosaur was and how its growth changed over the years.

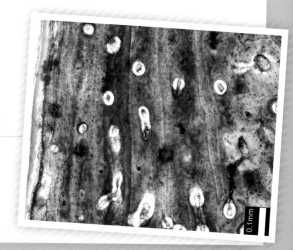

This is the inside of a dinosaur bone. It's cut super thin and seen under high magnification. Lines in the bone record when the dinosaur was growing slowly.

0.1mm

HEAD OF A LOVER, NOT A FIGHTER

Corythosaurus is named for its tall head crest, which looks like the battle helmet of a Corinthian warrior from ancient Greece. However, the crest of *Cory-thosaurus* wouldn't have been useful in a fight. It was hollow and made of thin bones. The crest looks like that of the modern cassowary, a large flightless bird from Australia and New Guinea. Cassowaries use their crests to attract mates. The same was probably true of *Corythosaurus*.

The crested Corinthian helmets of ancient Greece inspired the name *Corythosaurus*.

This is the skull of a cassowary, a modern flightless bird. It has a crest that is very similar to the crest of *Corythosaurus*.

BACK SUPPORT

These thin rod-like bones are called ossified tendons. Duck-billed and many other herbivorous dinosaurs have ossified tendons in their backs and tails. You have tendons in your spine too. They connect your vertebrae to your back muscles. They also help hold your spine together. However, your tendons are made of soft, stretchy tissues. The ossified tendons of dinosaurs were made of bone. These bony tendons helped to strengthen the spine. They kept the spine stiff, despite the dinosaur's great weight.

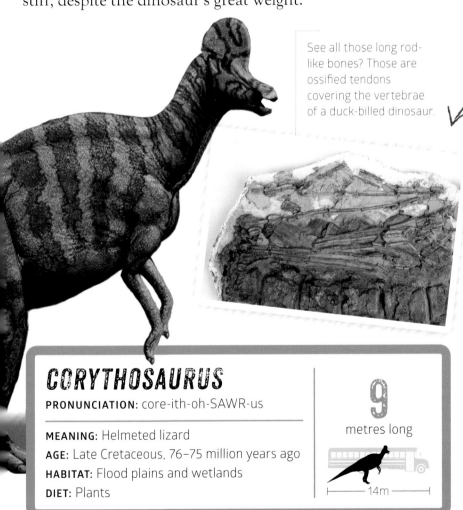

See all those long rod-like bones? Those are ossified tendons covering the vertebrae of a duck-billed dinosaur.

CORYTHOSAURUS

PRONUNCIATION: core-ith-oh-SAWR-us

MEANING: Helmeted lizard
AGE: Late Cretaceous, 76–75 million years ago
HABITAT: Flood plains and wetlands
DIET: Plants

9 metres long

⊢——— 14m ———⊣

MASTER CHEWERS

Hadrosaurs and ceratopsians were once Alberta's top herbi-vores. Key to their success was their ability to chew. Hadro-saurs and ceratopsians had beaks in the front of their snouts for nipping off leaves and small branches. Behind their beaks were fleshy cheeks and teeth. The individual teeth of hadrosaurs and ceratopsians were small. But the teeth grew in large, tightly packed groups called **dental batteries**. These dental batteries formed big grinding surfaces. They stayed in peak chewing form, because new teeth were always growing in from below to replace worn-down teeth. With beaks and dental batteries, hadrosaurs and ceratopsians mowed their way across the Cretaceous landscape.

CRUSHING AND MUNCHING, SLICING AND DICING

Although hadrosaurs and ceratopsians both had dental batteries, the two groups chewed in different ways. Compare these ceratopsian and hadrosaur teeth.

The ceratopsian tooth is bigger. It also has two roots. The smaller hadrosaur tooth has only one root. Double roots gave ceratopsian teeth a stronger anchor in the jaws.

Root

This tooth belongs to a hadrosaur. Notice that it has only one root.

Root

This tooth belongs to a ceratopsian. Notice that it has two roots.

In this hadrosaur jaw you can see tightly packed teeth that form a dental battery.

Now, look closely at these ceratopsian and hadrosaur lower jaws.

The ceratopsian dental battery is only one tooth wide. The hadrosaur battery contains many rows of teeth. So the grinding surfaces of hadrosaur batteries were much larger. But that's not all. You can see that the grinding surface of the hadrosaur battery is flat and straight across the jaw. Upper and lower hadrosaur teeth met one on top of the other, just like yours do. Hadrosaur chewing resembled that of modern mammals. But now look at the grinding surface of the ceratopsian battery. It's slanted. So ceratopsian upper and lower teeth slid across each other at an angle. Ceratopsian chewing resembled the shearing of two scissor blades.

Ceratopsian jaws had big beaks in the front and lots of teeth in the back.

Chapter 4

DINOSAURS IN MOTION

Sitting Ducks?

When it comes to avoiding predators, small animals have more options than big ones. Little creatures can hide in all kinds of tiny spots. They may also be able to find safety in trees or burrows. However, when you're an animal the size of a rhinoceros or an elephant, there aren't many places you can hide. Climbing trees or digging burrows is impossible.

Rearing back onto its hind legs, the duckbill *Brachylophosaurus* runs for its life. The tyrannosaur *Daspletosaurus* has ambushed it!

Large herbivorous dinosaurs had this problem. They were hunted by tyrannosaurs and other big carnivores, and couldn't just stay out of sight. They had to evolve different ways to avoid being eaten. The ceratopsians evolved horns, making them too dangerous to attack head-on. The ankylosaurs evolved spiky, bony plates, giving themselves suits of armour. What about the hadrosaurs? How did they protect themselves? Duck-billed dinosaurs had no armour or weapons and were bigger than pickup trucks. They seem to have been easy targets. But hadrosaurs were some of the most common and successful of all herbivorous dinosaurs.

Although they could not hide, maybe hadrosaurs could run. This would explain the group's lack of heavy armour and horns. Could a fleeing duckbill really outrun a tyrannosaur? Paleontologists have discovered the answer. You can follow the clues to solve the puzzle yourself.

Running Tall

When walking and grazing, duck-billed dinosaurs used their front limbs to help support their weight. They stood in a quadrupedal (four-legged) stance. However, the arms of hadrosaurs were much shorter and weaker than their back legs. When hadrosaurs needed to run, they reared back and stood in a bipedal (two-legged) stance. Running on just their back legs helped hadrosaurs take longer and more powerful strides. Tyrannosaurs also ran on their two back legs.

The hands of hadrosaurs were much smaller than their back feet. Hadrosaur hands helped them hold up their bodies when walking slowly. But hadrosaurs would rise onto only their back legs when running.

Leggy Tyrants

In your skeleton, **metatarsals** are the bones between your toes and ankle. Dinosaurs also had metatarsals. But they did not walk the same way we humans do. Dinosaurs stood only on their toes, so their metatarsals were held up off the ground. This is an important difference. It means that the metatarsals are part of a dinosaur's leg. Leg length is important when it comes to running. The longer a dinosaur's legs, the more ground it can cover with each step. Covering a lot of ground helps you move faster.

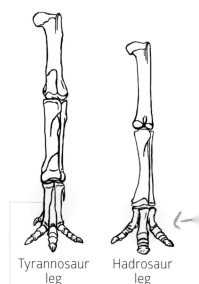

Tyrannosaur leg   Hadrosaur leg

The upper leg bones of *Tyrannosaurus* (left) aren't much longer than those of the duckbill *Edmontosaurus* (right). It's the lower leg bones, especially the metatarsals, that give tyrannosaurs longer legs.

Compare the size of the metatarsals in the leg of a large hadrosaur and a tyrannosaur. The tyrannosaur metatarsal is longer. This means that the tyrannosaur had a slightly longer leg. It was probably faster than a hadrosaur. Tyrannosaur metatarsals were also adapted for speed in another way.

Firm Footing

The metatarsals of tyrannosaurs were long. They were also oddly shaped. In most dinosaurs, the middle metatarsal was the largest and the thickest. However, tyrannosaur middle metatarsals were thin and wedge-shaped.

Look at this *Tyrannosaurus* foot. You can see that the odd shape makes the middle metatarsal fit tightly together with the others. Paleontologists have discovered that this tight fit was extremely good at enduring strong up-and-down forces. Exactly the sort of forces the metatarsal would have faced when tyrannosaurs were sprinting and making sharp turns. So tyrannosaurs were specially evolved for speed and agility.

Tail Ends

These vertebrae come from near the tips of tyrannosaur and hadrosaur tails. Neither hadrosaurs nor tyrannosaurs had a lot of muscle close to the tail tip. Still, tyrannosaur tail vertebrae might have helped tyrannosaurs move. Notice that the tyrannosaur tail vertebrae are longer than those of the hadrosaur. The tyrannosaur vertebrae also have longer bits of bone that point towards the rear and front. These pointy bone bits are small, but they have a long name. They are called zygapophyses. Zygapophyses connect with the other tail vertebrae in front of and behind them. These connections stiffened the tail. The stiff end of a tyrannosaur tail could have swung quickly from side to side. This would have helped with balance when making sharp turns.

These vertebrae come from near the end of a tyrannosaur (left) and hadrosaur (right) tail. The tyrannosaur vertebra is long and thin. The hadrosaur vertebra is short and squat.

Dr. Scott Persons
More Than Junk in the Trunk

A lot of things affect how fast different kinds of dinosaurs could run. Leg bones are only part of the story. Leg muscles are also important. In humans and most mammals, most of our running power comes from the muscles in our butts and thighs. Dinosaurs were different. Most dinosaurs got their running power from a big muscle in their tail. That muscle is called the **caudofemoralis**.

Think for a moment about the tails of large modern land mammals. Picture the rear of a horse, cow, elephant or giraffe. These mammals do not have caudofemoralis muscles. Compared to dinosaurs, they all have tails that are downright puny, only good for swatting flies. Instead, we need to look at the tails of modern reptiles. Lizards and crocodiles do have caudofemoralis muscles. They also tend to have large and muscular tails.

I began my research on dinosaur tail muscles by cutting up (dissecting) the tails of many types of reptiles. I looked at where and how the tail muscles attached to the tail and leg bones. I learned how the size of the caudofemoralis and the shape of the tail bones are related. Then I carefully measured the tail bones of dinosaurs. I used these measurements to build computer models of

the dinosaur tail skeletons. Finally, using what I had learned about tail muscles from the modern reptiles and the computer models, I recreated the size of dinosaurs' tail muscles. When I was done, I got a big surprise. The caudofemoralis of both tyrannosaurs and hadrosaurs turned out to be supersized.

To learn about tail muscles, I dissected lots of modern reptiles, including this caiman (a relative of crocodiles).

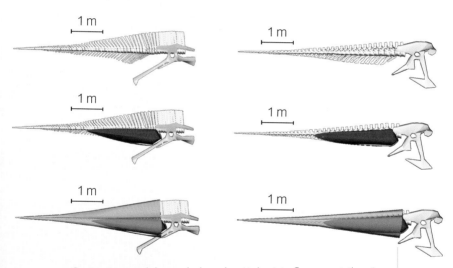

Computer models can help paleontologists figure out the size of dinosaur tail muscles. The three models on the left show a hadrosaur, and the three on the right show a tyrannosaur. The size and shape of different parts of the tail and hip skeleton (top row) indicate the size and shape of the muscles that attached to them. The caudofemoralis muscle of the hadrosaur and tyrannosaur is modelled in red (middle row). The other tail muscles are modelled overtop (bottom row), showing just how beefy dinosaur tails were.

Beefing Up the Back End

Albertosaurus   Lambeosaurus

fourth trochanter

Hadrosaurs had fourth trochanters much farther down their legs. This made the pull of hadrosaur tail muscles slower but easier.

Tyrannosaurs and hadrosaurs had extremely large caudofemoralis muscles. These leg-powering muscles were much larger than those in most other types of dinosaurs and all modern reptiles. However, the skeletons of tyrannosaurs and hadrosaurs evolved to support a large caudofemoralis in two very different ways.

The big bone between the hip and the knee is called the **femur**.

The femur on the left belongs to a tyrannosaur. The one on the right belongs to a hadrosaur. Both have a crest where the caudofemoralis attaches. This attachment crest is called the **fourth trochanter**. On the hadrosaur femur, the fourth trochanter is near the middle of the femur. On the tyrannosaur femur, the fourth trochanter is higher, nearer the hip.

Now, look at this hadrosaur tail vertebra. You can see several bony bits that stick out. On top is a long piece of bone with a hole at its base. This is the spinous process. Nerves run through the hole. Sticking out on the left and right sides are the caudal ribs. Lastly, the Y-shaped bone at the bottom is called the **chevron**. On a single tail vertebra, the caudofemoralis filled the space below the caudal ribs and down to the bottom tip of the chevron. Hadrosaurs evolved long chevrons, much longer than those of tyrannosaurs. So the big caudofemoralis of hadrosaurs evolved to be low. Tyrannosaurs and many of their carnivorous relatives evolved the opposite way. They raised their caudal ribs. So their big caudofemoralis was high.

spinous process

caudal rib

chevron

This vertebra and chevron belong to the tail of the hadrosaur *Edmontosaurus*.

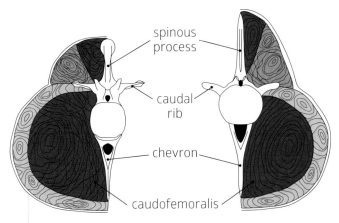

spinous process

caudal rib

chevron

caudofemoralis

Tyrannosaur

Hadrosaur

To understand the muscles and bones inside a live dinosaur's tail, imagine we could cut one, just like chopping a carrot. Looking at one of these slices, this is what you would see. Notice that the caudal ribs of the tyrannosaur are higher and the caudofemoralis is taller. The chevron of the hadrosaur sticks down farther and the caudofemoralis is deeper.

Runners, take your marks. Imagine a race between a hadrosaur and a tyrannosaur.

Dino Derby

Suppose you had to place a bet on a race between a hadrosaur and a tyrannosaur. Based on what you have seen so far, which dino racer do you think would win? Both run on their hind legs and are powered by extremely large caudofemoralis muscles. However, in the tyrannosaur, the caudofemoralis is high, and in the hadrosaur, the caudofemoralis is low. This difference is important. It means that the winner of the race would probably depend on how long the race is.

Quick and Deadly

Bang! The race begins. With longer legs and stronger metatarsals, the tyrannosaur takes an early lead. The tyrannosaur has another advantage that helps it leave the hadrosaur in a cloud of dust. As the tyrannosaur runs, its legs swing back and forth. Think for a moment about your legs when they swing. A good long swing will bring your foot a good long distance. How about your knee? It is farther up your leg, so it doesn't swing as far. In the tyrannosaur, the fourth trochanter is high. So it swings only a short distance. This means the tyrannosaur's caudofemoralis needs to pull only a short distance to fully power each step. Each short pull takes only a short amount of time. This lets the tyrannosaur swing its legs faster. Like a modern lion or cheetah, the tyrannosaur is capable of sudden bursts of high speed.

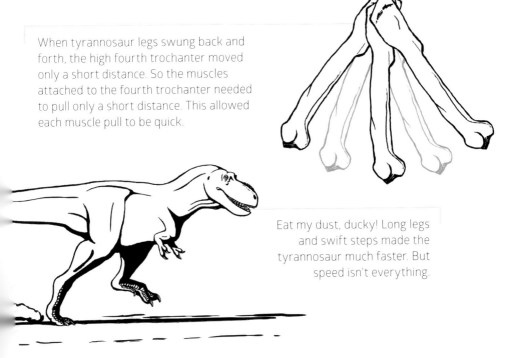

When tyrannosaur legs swung back and forth, the high fourth trochanter moved only a short distance. So the muscles attached to the fourth trochanter needed to pull only a short distance. This allowed each muscle pull to be quick.

Eat my dust, ducky! Long legs and swift steps made the tyrannosaur much faster. But speed isn't everything.

The hadrosaur has better endurance. In a long race, the tyrannosaur tires out first.

Slow and Steady

What if the race wasn't just a short dash? What if it was a full lap or two around the track? The tyrannosaur charges out of the starting gate at a breakneck speed. But the carnivore cannot maintain the pace. The tyrannosaur starts to slow. Its breathing becomes heavy. Its big caudofemoralis aches from the effort. Meanwhile, the hadrosaur steadily closes the gap. In the home stretch, the duckbill still shows no signs of tiring. It passes the tyrannosaur.

The lower fourth trochanter of the hadrosaur needs a longer and slower pull. But the lower position makes those

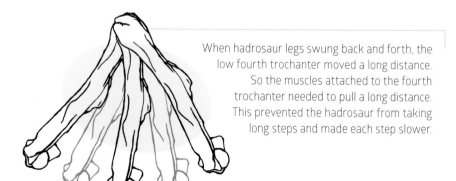

When hadrosaur legs swung back and forth, the low fourth trochanter moved a long distance. So the muscles attached to the fourth trochanter needed to pull a long distance. This prevented the hadrosaur from taking long steps and made each step slower.

pulls much easier. To understand why, you can do a quick experiment with a swinging cupboard door. Go try to pull the door closed by grabbing it first far away from the hinges and then close to the hinges. You will find that pulling from near the hinges is a lot harder. If it is a heavy door, you will tire your muscles out quickly. Although the tyrannosaur can run much faster, the hadrosaur has better endurance.

Dinosaur Zebras

Is endurance running a good way to avoid predators? Can it explain how the unarmed and unarmoured hadrosaurs survived? Modern zebras on the savannahs of Africa use endurance running to stay alive. Even though they don't have any horns or armour, zebras are one of the most common big African animals. Adult zebras are pretty fast. They can run at up to 56 kilometres an hour. But many of their predators—including lions and cheetahs—can run at up to 80 and 110 kilometres an hour. Still, zebras are able to avoid becoming a meal. Their predators can only run for short distances before getting tired. All zebras need to do is stay alert and avoid letting a big cat creep into striking range. To help guard against sneak attacks, zebras live in herds. A herd's many watchful eyes can keep a sharp lookout. Like zebras, hadrosaurs also lived in large herds. Perhaps endurance running was an even better strategy for hadrosaurs than it is for zebras. Zebras must watch out for stealthy cats. Hadrosaurs only had to spot tyrannosaurs, which were the size of billboards.

Chapter 5:

BEYOND EXTINCTION

Dinosaurs of a Feather

For more than 100 years, paleontologists argued about where birds came from. Some thought birds had evolved from dinosaurs. Others thought birds had evolved from another kind of prehistoric reptile, perhaps a relative of crocodiles. Over the years, more and more fossils were found. The debate is now over.

Lots of dinosaurs don't look much like birds. It's hard to believe *Triceratops* and *Stegosaurus* are close relatives of hummingbirds and penguins. And they're not. Birds didn't evolve from ceratopsians or thyreophorans. They evolved from a special branch of the theropod dinosaur family tree. On this branch, there are many dinosaurs that do look a lot like birds. These dinosaurs have feet with one toe that points backwards and three forward-pointing toes, just like birds. They have S-curved necks and wishbones, just like birds. They have vertebrae filled with tiny sacs of air, just like birds. Some have wrists that can fold backwards and big breastbones, just like birds. And some, including *Velociraptor* and close relatives of *Tyrannosaurus*, share the most bird-like of all traits: feathers.

Dino Fuzz

On my first dinosaur dig in Alberta, my team made a surprising discovery. We found a specimen of the theropod *Ornithomimus*. *Ornithomimus* is not a rare dinosaur to find, but there was more to our specimen than just a skeleton. There was also a coat of fossil feathers. These dinosaur feathers did not look much like the long leaf-shaped wing feathers of modern birds. Instead, they were short and hair-like. *Ornithomimus* couldn't fly. Its fuzzy hair-like covering shows that feathers first evolved for some reason other than flight. The feathers of *Ornithomimus*, and many other dinosaurs, probably helped hold in body heat, like the fur coats of mammals.

ORNITHOMIMUS

PRONUNCIATION:
or-nith-oh-MY-mus

MEANING: Bird mimic

AGE: Late Cretaceous,
76.5–66.5 million years ago

HABITAT: Flood plains
and wetlands

DIET: Plants

4 metres long

6m

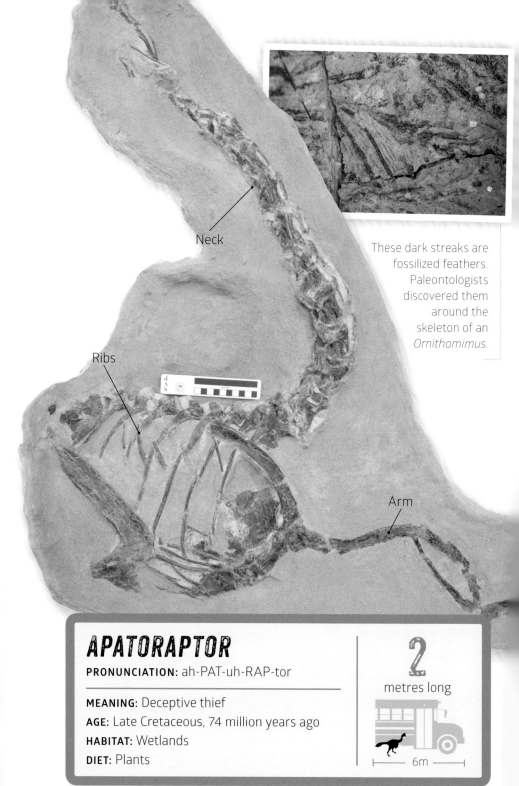

Neck

Ribs

Arm

These dark streaks are fossilized feathers. Paleontologists discovered them around the skeleton of an *Ornithomimus*.

APATORAPTOR

PRONUNCIATION: ah-PAT-uh-RAP-tor

MEANING: Deceptive thief
AGE: Late Cretaceous, 74 million years ago
HABITAT: Wetlands
DIET: Plants

2 metres long

6m

Shake Your Tail Feathers

To keep dinosaurs warm, early feathers only needed to be simple and hair-like. But more complex leaf-shaped feathers have also been found on dinosaurs that couldn't fly. **Oviraptorosaurs** are one example. They grew complex feathers on their arms and the end of their tail. These complex feathers formed large fans. What good were they? Paleontologists discovered that oviraptorosaurs' tails were muscular and flexible. So oviraptorosaurs could really shake and waggle their tail feathers. Like modern peacocks and turkeys, oviraptorosaurs probably used their feather fans to help show off during mating dances.

Hen's Teeth

The first birds evolved from theropod dinosaurs in the Jurassic Period. By the Cretaceous, dinosaurs had been living alongside birds for millions of years. *Ichthyornis* was one of these Cretaceous birds. It looked a lot like a modern seagull. Like a

ICHTHYORNIS

PRONUNCIATION: ICK-thee-OR-nis

MEANING: Fish bird
AGE: Late Cretaceous, 93–84 million years ago
HABITAT: Coastal shorelines
DIET: Fish

0.8
metre wingspan   ⊢——— 6m ———⊣

Dr. Ryan McKellar
Buried Feathers

Amber is fossilized tree **resin**. Resin is sticky, and creatures often get stuck in it. When resin hardens and fossilizes, anything stuck in it fossilizes too. Scientists have found insects, spiders, flower petals and even whole frogs and lizards inside amber.

In 2011, Dr. Ryan McKellar discovered fossilized feathers in amber excavated from southern Alberta. Some of the amber-covered feathers seem to have come from prehistoric birds. Other feathers have a simpler shape. This shows they came from non-avian dinosaurs. Before this discovery, the only known dinosaur feathers were flattened fossils. Dr. McKellar's amber feathers showed us the first 3-D view of early feathers. They also show colour patterns.

These dinosaur feathers are fossilized inside a nugget of amber.

Within this piece of amber, you can see very simple hair-like feathers. Look closer and you can also see that the feathers are speckled. This is a rare glimpse of dinosaur colour.

gull, *Ichthyornis* had long feathered wings that it used to soar on sea breezes. It swooped down to catch fish. It had long toe bones, and its feet were probably webbed. So it was also a good swimmer. Just as many dinosaurs show traits that were once thought to be unique to birds, so do many prehistoric birds show traits that birds were once thought to lack. Unlike any seagull or other modern bird, *Ichthyornis* had jaws filled with small sharp teeth.

Death from Above
The Asteroid That (Almost) Killed the Dinosaurs

Sixty-six million years ago, big carnivorous and herbivorous dinosaurs lived on every continent. Pterosaurs flew through the skies. Big mosasaurs and plesiosaurs swam in the oceans. Then a mass extinction wiped out most dinosaurs and other big Cretaceous reptiles. For years, paleontologists have tried to figure out what happened. Now we think we know the answer.

If you go to the very oldest Cretaceous rock layers in Alberta, you will see something out of this world. There is a grey streak in the rocks. To see the streak, you don't have to be in Alberta. You can go anywhere with rock layers that are 66 million years old. The streak is all over the world. What caused it? The streak is a thin layer made of a metal called iridium. Iridium is very rare on the surface of the earth, but is very common in asteroids. Scientists wondered how so much space metal ended up scattered in a layer all over Earth. The answer was surprising.

At the end of the Cretaceous, a huge asteroid hit Earth.

The powerful crash exploded most of the asteroid into fine dust. A lot of dust filled the earth's skies. Eventually, the dust floated down out of the atmosphere and settled to the ground. The dark streak is this layer of asteroid dust.

Obviously, the asteroid was bad news for any dinosaurs that happened to be standing under it when it fell. But how did it kill off so many dinosaurs and other animals all over the planet? Some larger and very hot chunks of rock were flung up from the crash. These burning rock chunks may have caused forest fires where they fell. The crash also created huge tidal waves in the ocean. These tidal waves struck land and caused sudden floods. But the real lethal weapon was the dust itself. It took many years before all that dust floated down out of the atmosphere. While it was still up there, it covered the earth in thick smog. The smog blocked both the light and the heat from the sun. Less light and sudden permanent cold weather caused plants to die. Then animals that ate plants starved. Most small herbivores died off, but it was especially bad for big herbivores. Big herbivores, which in the Cretaceous were nearly all dinosaurs, needed to eat large amounts of plants. Without lots of herbivores to eat, big meat eaters went extinct as well.

Dinosaur Survivors

When the dust from the asteroid collision finally settled, many small animals did survive. But sauropodomorphs, thyreophorans, ceratopsians, pachycephalosaurs, ornithopods and tyrannosaurs were all gone. Still, it's wrong to say that all dinosaurs are extinct. The asteroid collision killed off most but not all dinosaurs. One group made it through. In fact, there are more than 10,000 species of living dinosaurs: birds.

In 1977, the province of Alberta asked children to vote on the official provincial bird. The kids chose *Bubo virginianus*—the great horned owl. This also makes the great horned owl the official provincial dinosaur.

BUBO

(horned owl)

PRONUNCIATION: BOO-bow

MEANING: Owl

AGE: Quaternary,
2–0 million years ago

HABITAT: Woodlands

DIET: Small mammals, reptiles, birds and invertebrates

2 metre wingspan

6m

WHAT COMES NEXT?

More to Discover

It's an exciting time to be a paleontologist. How much we know about dinosaurs is increasing fast. There are more museums, more dinosaur research programs and more paleontologists than ever before. But there's still much left to learn. We now know that many dinosaurs had feathers. But we don't know if the very first dinosaurs had feathers or if feathers only evolved in later dinosaurs. We know that even big dinosaurs hatched from relatively small eggs and that many baby dinosaurs lived side by side with their parents. But we don't know if baby dinosaurs ate the same foods as adults or if dinosaur diets changed as they grew. We now have an explanation for why dinosaurs (except for birds) became extinct. But we don't yet understand why dinosaurs became so successful to begin with. These are interesting questions. It will take the work of paleontologists in Alberta and all over the world to answer them.

Paleontologists think that more than 99 per cent of all the species of dinosaurs that ever lived haven't been discovered yet. Some of those species may not have fossilized. We may never know what they were like. But many others probably did leave behind fossils. We just have to find them.

Join the Hunt

Think you might want to become a paleontologist? I decided that I wanted to be one when I was two and a half years old. I never changed my mind. Being a paleontologist isn't easy. You have to work hard in the dust and dirt and heat of the badlands. You have to take very careful measurements and research notes. And you have to spend lots and lots of time reading, writing and studying. Still, there is no thrill like unearthing a fossil that's been buried for tens of millions of years. Or being the very first person to learn something new about the life or evolution of a prehistoric beast. As a paleontologist, I have travelled the world. I have found fossils in the deserts of Mongolia, the plains of Patagonia and the savannahs of Africa. There's nothing else I would rather do. If you feel the same way, here are some tips to help you get there:

I always wanted to be a paleontologist. This is me as a kid teaching some classmates about *Velociraptor.*

WHAT TO STUDY IN SCHOOL

Reading and Writing – Science is all about sharing new ideas and information with other scientists. To do that, you need to be able to read and write scientific reports and papers.

Biology and Geology – Paleontology is a combination of these two types of science. Biology is the science of life. Geology is the science of rocks, erosion and the history of the earth.

Math – Calculations and measurements are a part of every paleontological study. To be a good paleontologist you will need math skills.

WHERE TO LEARN MORE

Natural History Museums – Museums are the place to see real fossils. Next time you visit a museum, try to identify some of the dinosaurs from this book. Look for some of the traits you have read about.

Websites – There are lots of great places online to learn about dinosaurs. Here are three of my favourites:

The Houston Museum of Natural Science's BEYONDbones blog (Look for the posts by my friend Dr. Robert Bakker.)
blog.hmns.org/category/paleontology/
National Geographic's Prehistoric World (This is a great place to learn about prehistoric life from across the globe.)
www.nationalgeographic.com/science/the-prehistoric-world/
DKfindout!'s Dinosaurs and Prehistoric Life (I really like their interactive dinosaur images.)
www.dkfindout.com/us/dinosaurs-and-prehistoric-life/

Libraries – When I was little, my dad took me to the library every week. You can check out other dinosaur books there, and many libraries have public science programs and events.

Zoos – As you have read, paleontologists often use modern animals to figure out how dinosaurs lived. The next time you are at the zoo, notice how the animals there are different from each other. Think about how those differences are related to how they live. Understanding the present is often the key to understanding the past.

GLOSSARY

Bold within a glossary definition means the word is also defined in the glossary.

Adaptation: a **trait** that has evolved to help a species survive and reproduce in a particular way.

Amber: fossilized tree **resin**. Amber often contains the **fossils** of insects and other creatures that got stuck in the resin before it hardened. Amber is also a gemstone.

Ankylosaurids: a group of **ankylosaur** dinosaurs with horns and tail clubs.

Ankylosaurs: a group of **thyreophoran** dinosaurs with armoured skulls and a covering of **osteoderms** across their bodies. There are two major kinds of ankylosaurs: **ankylosaurids** and **nodosaurids**.

Atmosphere: the gas that surrounds a planet.

Badlands: a dry hilly environment with few plants. In badlands, **erosion** has carved many small canyons and gullies through the hillsides. These eroded hillsides often contain many rock layers and lots of **fossils**.

Bonebed: a specific area filled with lots of **fossil** bones. Some bonebeds are small concentrations of fossils, but others can stretch for many kilometres.

Carnivorous: meat-eating.

Caudofemoralis: a large muscle behind the hips and along the tails of dinosaurs, reptiles and some amphibians. The caudofemoralis is attached to the femur. It helps dinosaurs move their back legs.

Cenozoic Era: the chunk of time from 65.5 million years ago to the present. The Cenozoic Era is also known as the Age of Mammals. **Mammals** first evolved in the **Mesozoic**. But during the Cenozoic, they began to grow large.

Ceratopsians: a group of four-legged **herbivorous** dinosaurs. Most ceratopsians have horns and large neck shields.

Champsosaurs: a group of prehistoric aquatic reptiles with long narrow jaws.

Chevron: a type of tail bone. Chevrons sit below the spine. Chevrons provide attachments for tail muscles and also protect large blood paths.

Coprolite: fossilized poop.

Cretaceous Period: the chunk of time between 145 to 65.5 million years ago. The Cretaceous is the last period in the **Mesozoic Era**. (See also **Late Cretaceous**.)

Deinonychosaurs: a **carnivorous** group of **theropod** dinosaurs. They're also known as raptors. Deinonychosaurs had large foot claws and were closely related to birds.

Dental batteries: large chewing surfaces formed by tightly packed teeth. Dental batteries evolved in **hadrosaur** and **ceratopsian** dinosaurs.

Denticles: the tiny sharp bumps that form the **serrated edges** of teeth. When an animal bites, denticles help a tooth to cut. Lots of pressure is applied to the tips of the bumps, rather than being spread across the whole edge.

Ecosystem: an environment and all the life that lives within it.

Enamel: the hard, shiny material that usually covers the outside of teeth.

Erosion: the process of rocks wearing down into sediments. Erosion is often caused slowly by weak forces, like rain or wind. But sometimes it can be caused suddenly by powerful forces, like floods or volcanic eruptions.

Evolution: the process of species accumulating new **adaptations** over time and of one species changing into a new one.

Excavating: digging up **fossils**. Excavating a large fossil usually involves using big tools, like shovels and pickaxes, to dig around the fossil. **Paleontologists** also use very small tools, like brushes and hand picks, to dig close to it.

Femur: the large leg bone between the hip and knee.

Fossils: objects from the past that tell us about prehistoric life. Often, fossils are bones, teeth or other hard parts of an animal's body. Most fossils have lasted for millions of years because they were buried safely underground.

Fourth trochanter: a crest of bone on the **femur**. The **caudofemoralis** attaches to the fourth trochanter. Animals that don't have a caudofemoralis also don't have a fourth trochanter.

Geologist: a person who studies rocks and the processes that change the shape of the earth. Some of these processes include volcanic eruptions, **erosion** and drifting continents.

Greenhouse climate: a warm climate that results from gases in the **atmosphere**. These gases allow heat from the sun to pass through to Earth's surface but prevent the heat from escaping back out to space.

Hadrosaurs: a group of **ornithopod** dinosaurs with large broad beaks and **dental batteries**.

Half rings: special bones from the necks of **ankylosaurs**. Half rings are crescent shaped and have spiky **osteoderms** that help protect the neck.

Herbivorous: plant-eating.

Ichthyosaurs: a group of prehistoric marine reptiles with fish-like bodies.

Jurassic Period: the chunk of time between 201 and 145 million years ago. The Jurassic is the middle period of the **Mesozoic Era**.

Keratin: a tough material that covers the outside of claws, horns and beaks. Feathers, hair and scales are also made of keratin.

Late Cretaceous: a span of time within the **Cretaceous Period**. It's the chunk of time between 100.5 and 65.5 million years ago.

Mammals: animals that produce milk, have a constant body temperature and usually have hair. Some modern mammals are humans, dogs, whales, rodents and kangaroos.

Mesozoic Era: a chunk of time between 252 and 66 million years ago. The

Mesozoic Era is also known as the Age of Dinosaurs. Dinosaurs first evolved in the Mesozoic. At the end of the Mesozoic, all non-avian dinosaurs went extinct.

Metatarsals: long bones in the feet between the ankle and toes.

Microsite: a place with many small **fossils**.

Migration: the journey of an animal from one place to another and then back again as the seasons change.

Mineralization: the process of becoming filled with minerals. Mineralization occurs after a **fossil** is buried. Tiny crystals slowly grow inside a fossil's hollow spaces.

Monospecific bonebed: a site filled with **fossil** bones that mostly belong to a single species.

Mosasaurs: a group of prehistoric marine lizards with flippers and tail fins.

Nodosaurids: a group of **ankylosaur** dinosaurs with narrow snouts and without tail clubs.

Ontogeny: the study of how a creature changes as it grows up.

Ornithomimids: a **herbivorous** group of **theropod** dinosaurs. Ornithomimids are also known as the ostrich mimic dinosaurs. Ornithomimids had long legs and were some of the fastest dinosaurs.

Ornithopods: a group of two-legged **herbivorous** dinosaurs.

Osteoderms: pieces of bony armour that grow in an animal's skin.

Oviraptorosaurs: a **herbivorous** group of **theropod** dinosaurs. Oviraptorosaurs had toothless beaks. Many had feather fans on their tails and arms.

Pachycephalosaurs: a group of two-legged **herbivorous** (and possibly omnivorous) dinosaurs with thick domed skulls.

Paleoecology: the study of prehistoric **ecosystems**.

Paleontologist: a person who studies prehistoric life.

Paleozoic Era: the chunk of time between 541 and 252.2 million years ago. The Paleozoic Era is also known as the Age of Fish, because fish first evolved during the Paleozoic. Fish have continued to diversify since the Paleozoic.

Pathologic: damaged by injury or sickness.

Phanerozoic Eon: the chunk of time between 541 million years ago and the present. The Phanerozoic Eon is also known as the Age of Life. During the Phanerozoic, large complex life forms became common and diverse.

Plesiosaurs: a group of prehistoric marine reptiles with short tails and large flippers. Some plesiosaurs had long necks with small heads. Others had large crocodile-like heads and short necks.

Preparators: people who clean **fossils** after they have been **excavated** in the field.

Pterosaurs: a group of flying reptiles closely related to dinosaurs. Pterosaurs had wings made of skin stretched from their legs and bodies to one very long finger on each hand. Pterosaurs first evolved in the Late **Triassic**. They went extinct at the end of the **Cretaceous Period**.

Radiometric dating: a method for figuring out how old a rock layer is by studying how many of its radioactive atoms have broken apart.

Resin: a sticky goo made by many plants. Resin helps plants heal by filling in broken or damaged parts of their woody stems or trunks. Resin also helps plants defend themselves from herbivores that are trying to eat them. Small herbivores, like insects, may become trapped in sticky resin. Larger herbivores usually don't like the taste or feel of resin stuck in their mouths. Fossilized resin is called **amber**.

Sauropodomorphs: a group of four-legged plant-eating dinosaurs with long necks. Some sauropodomorphs were the largest of all dinosaurs.

Scavengers: carnivores that eat animals that have been found dead, without having attacked or killed them.

Sediments: small pieces of rocks broken off by **erosion**. Sediments can be carried by fast-moving water. When the water slows, they often sink. Over time, sediments may pile up and harden together, forming a rock layer.

Serrated edge: a line of small sharp bumps (called **denticles**) on a tooth. Serrated edges help a tooth cut.

Stegosaurs: a group of **thyreophoran** dinosaurs. Stegosaurs have large spearhead-shaped **osteoderms** on their backs and spikes on their tails.

Syncervical: a special bone from the neck of a **ceratopsian**. Syncervicals are made of multiple neck **vertebrae** that have grown together into a single large bone. Syncervicals helped support the great weight of armoured ceratopsian skulls.

Tendons: tough bands that connect muscles to bones.

Trait: a characteristic of a species. Traits may be physical, like skin colour or the shape of a body part. They may also be a way of living, like burrowing, climbing or being nervous.

Theropods: a group of two-legged dinosaurs. The first theropods were **carnivorous**, and all carnivorous dinosaurs are theropods. However, many kinds of theropods, such as **oviraptorosaurs** and **ornithomimids**, are **herbivorous**.

Thyreophorans: a group of four-legged **herbivorous** dinosaurs with large **osteoderms** across their bodies.

Triassic Period: the chunk of time between 252 and 201 million years ago. The Triassic is the first period in the **Mesozoic Era**.

Tyrannosaurs: a group of **carnivorous theropod** dinosaurs. Tyrannosaurs had large skulls, thick teeth and small arms.

Vertebra: a bone from the neck, back or tail. Vertebrae string together to form the spinal column.

INDEX

About the Authors

DR. W. SCOTT PERSONS IV is a paleontologist and instructor at the University of Alberta. He has taken part in fossil-hunting expeditions throughout the badlands of the American West, the Gobi Desert of Mongolia, the canyons of Tanzania's Olduvai Gorge, the pampas of Argentina and the volcanic ash beds of northern China. His work has been featured on the National Geographic and Discovery channels and in *Smithsonian* and *Discover* magazines. He lives in Edmonton, AB.

DR. JULIUS T. CSOTONYI is a paleoartist and has collaborated on projects with several major museums and book publishers from around the globe, including the National Geographic Society and the Royal Tyrrell Museum. His artwork has appeared in numerous books including recently *The Paleoart of Julius Csotonyi* (Titan Books, 2014) and *Dinosaur Art: The World's Greatest Paleoart* (Titan Books, 2012). He has been honoured with the Society of Vertebrate Paleontology's Lanzendorf PaleoArt Prize for 2-Dimensional Art three times (2010, 2012, 2014). He lives in Vancouver, BC.